PRAISE

"It Was Her New York is like walking a different wavelength through the city and seeing a world outside the usual hubbub. With its unique sensitivity, it has an irresistible quietness."

—Jeremiah Moss, author of *Vanishing New York: How a Great City Lost Its Soul*

"This collection reveals an enduring New York with tough, zany, heartbreaking stories of these two women and all their fellow New Yorkers that capture the small details and great big soul of the city we love."

—Carola Dibbell, author of *The Only Ones* (an **Oprah Magazine** Favorite Book of the Year)

"Unflinchingly stark and brutally honest, but not at the expense of compassion, humor and a vibrancy of life, all captured with a thoughtful elegance."

—Joel Anderson Thompson, TV writer-producer of *House, Krypton, Superstition,* and *Roswell, New Mexico*

"The people of *It Was Her New York* survive and triumph in their city with an unconquerable spirit. They become a beacon of hope in this beautifully crafted world, one that is recognized and universally understood by all."

—Phillip Giambri, author of *The Amorous Adventures of Blondie and Boho: Two East Village Dive Bar Coyotes*

"Warning: Be prepared to laugh, cry, smile to yourself in recognition, and be overwhelmed by the lyrical language and the moving photos. It is the story of a New York childhood on the Lower East Side. It is the story of the pain of a mother's decline. It is the story of **Her** New York and once you read its sights, sounds and insights, it will be **Your** New York too."

—Deborah Edel, cofounder, Lesbian Herstory Archives

"What's it like to lose a cherished family member to old age and creeping dementia? What is it like to live in Manhattan and watch as the city of your youth also disappears as it becomes the primary province of the thoughtlessly rich? In *It Was Her New York*, C.O. Moed reveals her life and her mother's final years as she simultaneously paints the city with biting wit and a heartrending brush of memories so fresh and full of love and pain that you want to go to Coney Island with her right now."

—David Leaf (www.leafprod.com), Peabody and WGAW award-winning writer, director, and producer of **The U.S. vs John Lennon, The Night James Brown Saved Boston, Beautiful Dreamer: Brian Wilson & the Story of SMiLE,** UCLA professor and the author of *God Only Knows: The Story of Brian Wilson, the Beach Boys & The California Myth*

"Deep love is here for a mother and for streets filled with the history of people on the move. And a New York daughter's moxie is here too in words, pictures, and humor, attempting to keep loss in the wings for just a little longer."

—Joan Nestle, cofounder, Lesbian Herstory Archives

IT WAS HER NEW YORK

IT WAS HER NEW YORK

TRUE STORIES & SNAPSHOTS

C.O. MOED

Rootstock Publishing

Montpelier, VT

Release Date: February 29, 2024

Printed in the USA.

Published by Rootstock Publishing
an imprint of Ziggy Media LLC
Montpelier, Vermont 05602

info@rootstockpublishing.com
www.rootstockpublishing.com

ISBN: 978-1-57869-165-4

Library of Congress Number: 2023921128

eBook ISBN: 978-1-57869-166-1

Cover design by Sienna Long.

Book design by Eddie Vincent, ENC Graphics Services.

Author photo by Ted Krever.

For permissions or to schedule an author interview, contact the author at comoed@yahoo.com.

Dedicated to Florence

the Ex-Lover

and New York City

INTRODUCTION

Florence Deutsch Moed, aka Deutschie, wasn't suddenly incapacitated and in bedridden-land. There was no melodramatic movie scene where everything turns on a dime and the music swells. It wasn't even like a Hollywood blockbuster where everything explodes in the climatic big battle.

If only it were.

No. This was change by stealth.

Little by little the concert-trained Juilliard pianist who bore and raised my sister Louise and me began to disappear, one piano etude at a time, one word at a time, one memory at a time.

Little by little the city that raised us all—the one we grew up in, loved in, got lost in, could afford to live in—also began to disappear. One storefront at a time, one street at a time, one neighborhood at a time.

Yet, somehow, despite so-called urban progress and Florence's slow fade, the city and its girl stood their ground and refused to be erased. Welcome to Her New York.

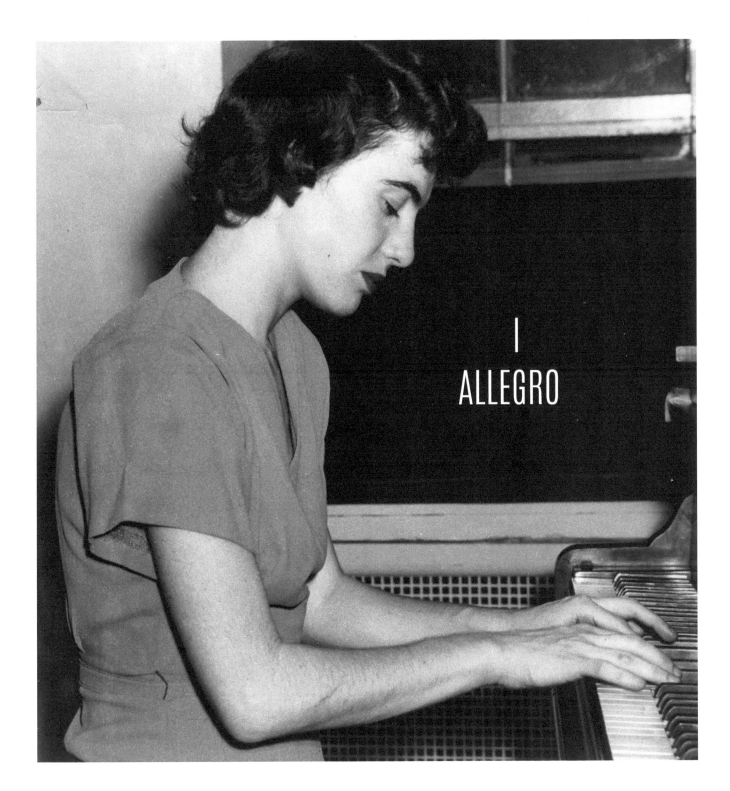

I

ALLEGRO

SINATRA'S DATING ADVICE

Florence is refusing to do much but lie in bed.

I say, "Fine. You don't want to get out of bed, then go lay down and die."

She yells, "Lie down! Not lay down! Lie down!"

I say, "You can't get out of bed, but you can still correct my grammar?"

She yells, "Yes! It matters!"

I yell, "THEN GET OUT OF BED!"

She doesn't.

I look at her butchered hair. It's butchered because a week ago, I took the household scissors and chopped off big chunks of it. I did that because it was a huge halo of wildness, so thick and silver sparkling. Now it is a huge halo of wildness that got caught in a buzz saw.

The Sunday afternoon *ALL THE JAZZ YOU CAN EAT* radio show begins.

We settle in to listen.

C.O. Moed

Sinatra comes on. He's wailing *Blues in the Night*.

Florence joins in. "Ooooo ... woman..... twooooo faces....cryinnnnngggg."

Knowing something of her dating history, I ask her if that's true.

She says, "I didn't make it up. That's what's written."

I start laughing. She asks why.

"You're singing with heart."

Shrugs. "I'm just trying to get the words."

And then she—who broke many hearts of many old girls and garnered many angry love letters and hurtful looks across crowded dances put on by the local gay and lesbian senior citizen's center—looks up and asks, "Is it true? A woman is two-faced?"

NEITHER SNOW NOR RAIN

NOR HEAT NOR GLOOM . . .

UNTIL SUDDENLY

None of us really understood that things were changing for Florence. She seemed as she always had been.

Teaching cooking walking arguing fuming eating investigating practicing devouring life . . . sallying forth into the world as the force of nature that she was.

The rare cracks were easy to ignore. More often than not they looked like the mishaps and mistakes we all make.

Until suddenly . . .

This was the first crack I couldn't ignore.

On the corner of Sixth Street and Avenue A. Heading home after teaching a piano student. Between her and the curb, a pile of snow dumped high from the recent storm.

Suddenly she couldn't traverse it. Suddenly she didn't know what to do.

Suddenly she was old.

And then suddenly some young men came up behind her, picked her up, carried her over the mound and gently placed her on solid sidewalk before vanishing into the crowd.

Telling me this on the phone after, she laughed and laughed and laughed about it because the joy of that sudden flight erased the sudden reality that she could no longer climb her own mountains.

C.O. Moed

SKATING ON THIN ICE

They were like dolphins, whooshing around me.

A woman I probably had once seen before at a dance or a demonstration or some revolutionary action maybe thirty years ago walked up to me as they zoomed by and said, "It's the invasion of the skateboards!"

I laughed. "I was thinking: 'Gee, I'd like to learn how to do that.'"

"Well, you know where to find them." She grinned as she walked away.

One of the kids stopped, skateboard propped on his sneaker. I snapped a picture.

"I think she just took your picture," another kid said under his breath.

"Yes. I did." I showed it to them.

"Are you going to post it somewhere?"

"Yeah."

"Like Instagram?"

"I'm old. I don't know what Instagram is." I started taking another picture and all the boys posed, gangsta-style.

"Oh please, cut the bullshit." It was funny, but not a picture. "I always wanted to learn how to skateboard, but when I was growing up, girls didn't. Now girls do. It's really cool."

"Yeah," one of them said, shrugging. All of them nodded like: What's the big deal? Some of the best skaters they knew were girls. That revolution was normal to them.

I lifted the phone to take another picture and one gave me a peace sign.

"What's that mean to you?" I asked.

"Peace," he said.

Crash noise that could only come from wood plank, metal wheels, and an iron fence that got in the way interrupted us.

"&#%!@?)," and then "&#%!@?) &#%!@?)" followed.

"Real peaceful," I said.

"He's not with us," the kid replied.

C.O. Moed

SNAP SHOTS FROM DEEP WATER: DIVING IN

Florence said that after my Gramma died, she started going to Coney Island "to make things right" and swim in honor of her mother.

Water was not a foreign entity on the Lower East Side. Not everybody swam, but everybody got wet—Coney or Pitt Street Pool or, in my aunts' and uncles' days, the East River.

I thought I had Pitt Street Pool conquered until one day the four feet of water wasn't four feet anymore and I found myself flailing. Either one of the bigger kids or my sister or a lifeguard pulled me out. The Educational Alliance day camp pool lessons taught me to float in case that happened again.

The Fourteenth Street Y had a pool and a teen program. At the age of thirteen, in a rare fit of acting my age, I badgered Florence for a bikini. It wasn't just the money, which was always tight, it was the risk of interrupting her slow fade into private desires and secret regrets—and suffering her ire.

But there was this boy and I was this girl and somehow I understood a bikini was part of the deal I wanted to make happen.

She caved, and with twenty dollars I headed off to A&S in Brooklyn. I don't remember the color, the style, the stripes, the dots. All I remember is rushing to the pool, seeing the boy I liked and jumping into the pool to say hello.

No one told me that, as I stood in freezing water trying to impress the object of my affection, the top of my bikini had slipped off my adolescent breasts.

Florence sewed the straps tighter, but I never wore it again. (I also refused to return to the Fourteenth Street Y for years and years. And when I did, this time as an oversize overall-wearing tax-paying adult, even then, I shook with humiliation.)

Then one day Gramma died, and Florence got on the F Train to Coney and dove into the ocean. I continued to stay dry with only a couple of interruptions here and there, like at the hundred-year-old City College pool or the elite NYU pool or some tiny hotel pool or a rare ocean vacation (but only up to my knees for fear of sharks). That was a long, long time ago.

As Florence began to swim in a haze of NPR and sheets of pee liner pads, occasionally coming up for air to say she hurt and was unhappy, out of the blue I enrolled—for the fifth or sixth time in twenty-five years—in adult beginner swimming lessons. There was even a sauna waiting for me at the end of an hour of breathing water up my nose.

When I told her I was learning to swim, rare delight, passion, and determination flooded her face. "Oh. You must."

C.O. Moed

RETURN TO THE PROMISED LAND

Shoes were serious business—after music, of course. That's where money was spent. A Good Pair That Would Last Forever. From the time she was a girl, when it rained and there were no galoshes to be had, Florence took off her shoes and walked barefoot. And on certain occasions, we all did.

Well, in those days there was just way less broken glass on the streets.

Florence hunted the clearance racks at the Herald Square Stride-Rite. But for us kids it was Kaplan's Shoes, on Clinton between Rivington and Stanton.

We went there for our once-a-year-pair-of-(ugly)-good-for-you-shoes that wouldn't become hip and fashionable for another twenty years.

In the interim, the meaner girls at PS 110 in their white go-go boots called me "Baby Shoes," which is devastating if you're only eight and in the fourth grade with the bigger kids.

The trip to Kaplan's was undertaken with the seriousness of a pilgrimage. There was a cat clock that wagged its tail and rolled its eyes to each ticking second. Very exotic compared to our bare-bones kitchen clock. The almost-leather seats were burgundy-something.

The so-called carpet was dusty and the lights were, of course, fluorescent. Only uptown stores where rich people shopped had real light fixtures with expensive light bulbs.

Florence's rule was, whatever ugly Oxford you picked at Kaplan's you had to wear out of the store. This showed commitment to the shoe you'd be with all year. And since that and the sneakers from Sears & Roebucks were the only things we bought new, you really had to know if the shoe fit.

The pressure was tough. But those ugly Oxfords were made so good and Mr. Kaplan's measurements were so precise, somehow everything worked out. Except for the part of looking like a dork from a-turn-of-the-century picture by Jacob Riis.

I spent the next forty years wearing high-heeled shit that looked hot, while avoiding any shoe stores that sold anything that was comfortable and good for your feet. But there is a God, and She does know shoes, because ugly came back into style and was even hipper than hip, especially with tight jeans.

Perfect timing. My feet were old and unhappy. It was time to find a place where the Oxfords were made so good and the measurements were so precise.

And when I walked into the dusty shoe store on Thirty-Ninth Street, it was just like returning home.

C.O. Moed

WE FALL IN FOUR LANGUAGES

Rush hour, everybody rushing home.

Except for the nicely dressed lady lying on the ground by Greeley Square. Between the serious men's clothing store and the Dunkin' Donuts.

There are a lot of people over her making sure her shopping bags and her purse are OK. There is a cup of something by her, and the security guy or police chief, or whatever he is, is talking into a walkie-talkie.

Me and two guys hang out on the curb by the flower pots and watch a skinny homeless guy shout at the crowd. He looks like the guy who kicked me in the ass when I bumped into him on a rainy day. Wouldn't be surprised if it was. This is his neighborhood.

The two guys said that she began to fall and the homeless guy caught her and was shouting "GET HELP GET HELP," and once non-homeless guys showed up and shooed him away he got upset. After all, he was there first and just because he was homeless didn't mean he was less of a hero.

The daily convoy of twenty-five blaring police cars roar up Sixth Avenue. None stop.

One of the guys I'm hanging with turns to me and shrugs. "She fell. Her heart, her blood pressure, or diabetic. Look, they give her an orange juice with some sugar. Look, she is fine."

A third man joins us. His patter sounds like poems made of rain on a roof. When I ask if it is Arabic, he nods. "I speak Danish too. And Spanish and English and Arabic," he says.

We look across the street at the woman again. Two ambulances come as she sits up and talks on her cell phone.

"We are nothing," The Danish-Spanish-English-Arabic-speaking guy says to no one in particular. "A heart or something and we fall . . . we are nothing."

C.O. Moed

GET READY, GET SET, GO

Literally, it was just yesterday Florence was on the Avenue D bus coming or going and stopping at nothing. When suddenly, something went terribly wrong. Her legs that carried her everywhere went kaput. And with that, we had an invalid mother. A really, really pissed-off invalid mother.

The hospital admitted her immediately. Louise thought it was maybe a broken hip, but the hip was fine. It was inside Florence's heart and brain that everything was broken. We just couldn't tell, because Florence's "broken" seemed so similar to Florence's normal.

She was a fall risk, so they had Hospital Companions who sat in the room all night making sure Florence didn't get out of bed at three a.m. and fall down.

That didn't go well.

One morning I found one Companion sitting outside the hospital room, refusing to go back in. Florence obviously had shared her opinion about that poor woman. It's tough being insulted and cursed at when it's not your mother.

Finally the hospital said, "You want your mother to go home? You need to set up twenty-four-hour care. Get cracking."

And, like the sudden hospital world, there was sudden paperwork, hundreds of lines to fill out, thousands of boxes to check and a million questions designed to destroy any chance of getting help. One social service person told me, "If you answer yes here but no here, we deny. If you answer yes here and here, we deny you. But if you answer no here and yes here, then . . . we deny you . . ."

After we wrote a very very very big check to a very very very good lawyer and a very very very good caseworker to get us help. I wondered what happened to other people who didn't have a mother who literally saved ninety cents of every dollar she made.

Maybe Florence knew that one day, suddenly, we would have to spend all the savings accounts she accrued because she rarely left a light on, never bought new clothes, only had coffee and maybe a sandwich when she "ate out" with the girls from the gay dances, didn't take fancy vacations—that's what Coney Island was for—maybe went on a plane three times, walked everywhere she could and bought discounted food, like day-old bread, bent cans and the loose grapes for a dollar sold at the Essex Street Market at the end of the day.

I wondered. And I kept wondering as I wrote every check—and every account got smaller and every form and documentation piled up—I wondered if all that down-to-the-bone living had been worth it.

C.O. Moed

MY SECRET GARDEN

If you wear headphones it's almost quiet.

In the middle there's a fountain and all these potted plants around it, so you almost think you're by a stream in a forest of palms and philodendron.

There are only a couple of benches.

Sometimes people pray in front of the statue of the Virgin Mother.

If you look up you can see the windows to the kitchen and the church workers washing their dishes.

**I SHOT MY SISTER
BUT I ONLY KILLED
HER A LITTLE**

It was bad, that week in November 1965.

In a rare moment of having the upper hand, I took my sister Louise's head and banged it hard against the baseboard of our sturdy couch. I was six. She was ten. In an hour she was in bed crying and in a week she was in the hospital with spinal meningitis.

I knew it was my fault. I tried to tell our parents, Florence and Seymour, that I was the cause of my sister being at death's door with thousands of needles stuck in her spine. But they were not known for having a listening ear, let alone comprehending the anguished fears of a little kid. So they may not have understood what I was trying to say.

A few days after my sister landed in the hospital, my father installed in the living room facing the Williamsburg Bridge an amazing

C.O. Moed

invention: a dimmer for the ceiling lamp that hung over the Steinway piano. That dimmer, like silk gowns in 1930s Fred and Ginger movies, ushered in light with luxurious elegance and grace. I was given strict instructions by my father never to touch it. Ever.

However, one night I found myself alone in the living room. My sister was in the hospital, my father somewhere in the mysterious travel between work and home, and Florence, oddly enough, not at her piano, a place she spent more time at than in the embrace of anyone who loved her. So, in a not-so-rare moment of refusing to follow orders, I decided to experience the power of the dimming.

I gently turned the knob right and the lights glowed. I gently turned it left and they faded. This was better than lighting matches in the bathroom sink! I turned the knob right again and the lights filled the room like a full moon. I turned the knob left again and the lights faded like a sunset. With a quick break to make sure Florence wasn't headed my way, I assured myself that one more time wouldn't hurt.

So I gently turned the knob right and the lights began to slowly glow, then suddenly the room went black. I froze in terror and then frantically began twisting the knob right and left and right and left, pleading with the ceiling lamp to work, when something outside the window caught my eye. Everything—the Williamsburg Bridge, all of Columbia Street, all the projects—everything that the eye could see was black.

Florence came stomping back from wherever she had been and went to the building's hallway. Neighbors' voices filled the stairs calling out to one another. Yes, it was true. There were no lights anywhere and no one knew why. But I did. Clearly, my act of disobeying my father had broken all the lights in New York City.

Shabbas candles came pouring out of the apartments, the stair banisters became a magic fairyland, and my father, hours later, found his way home by walking across the Bridge. But what I remember most from that night was being so strangled by guilt I clutched Florence's skirt and refused to let go until she, needing to pee, refused to let me go into the bathroom with her. So I stood outside the door and slowly died inside from the knowledge that this was the fate of a destroyer of sisters and cities—forever condemned to darkness.

The next day my parents and I walked up to Fifteenth Street and Second Avenue and waved up to my sister on the ninth or seventeenth floor of the hospital. She merrily waved back. Beth Israel had its own generator and she had been spared the dark.

Of course the 1965 Blackout happened because a bunch of rats were running around in some power station somewhere. My sister returned home well enough to continue being my sister, and nine months later a whole bunch of babies appeared on the street. And years after, the bad timing of my playing with the living room light dimmer made for a great dinner story to friends who didn't grow up in New York City and were easily impressed.

Then, one day, the Internet was invented and, shortly after that, someone introduced me to Google. Without even thinking, the first thing I looked up was causes of spinal meningitis. And there, in very clear language, after bacterial and viral causes, were these words: "a traumatic injury to the head or spine."

L aurel and Joyce's father grew up next door to my father in the tenements on Henry Street. Not the hip, overpriced, badly renovated, tons-of-cachet, faux-street-cred tenements of today, but the rat-filled, roach-saturated, filthy, overcrowded tenements of yesterday that earned the word *tenement*.

Their great-grandfather and grandfather had the stables down the street. They were the blacksmiths. Laurel and Joyce say it like it is, no bullshit. Maybe that came from the horses because you can't bullshit a horse.

My grandfather taught himself English, showed up to whatever work he could get, despite what we now suspect was depression, and was pro-union (although we suspect it was just an excuse to be self-righteous and punch other people besides his wife and kids). I think workers should be fairly paid for their work, and I've shown up to every job I could get, despite bona fide depression. Yeah, I got a temper, but unlike my grandfather, I keep it in check.

After the tenements got torn down and the co-ops got built, all our families got first dibs on fancy new apartments near one another. In

C.O. Moed

our world, fancy meant elevators, hot water, toilets inside the apartment, no rats, and less roaches. Lots of trees. Almost like Central Park.

Every once in a while, Laurel and Joyce's mom, Dolly, would say, "Let's go visit Florence," and they would come over and sit at the kitchen table, watching the trains going back and forth on the Williamsburg Bridge. Both of them knew the plaid "lumberjack" jacket from L.L.Bean and the Keds sneakers Florence always wore. No one in the neighborhood looked like her. I mean, she really stuck out. So it made sense Laurel and Joyce would remember Florence so well.

They also knew we all walked everywhere. Spending carfare was a very serious decision, and if it wasn't necessary then we didn't. And by necessary, I mean unless the destination was more than an hour away by foot, the answer was no. Even if it wasn't—like Gramma's—we had to walk back.

Laurel and Joyce still live in the old neighborhood that was built on top of the old-old neighborhood. I went downtown for tea and talk and picture-looking-at. As I walked in the door, Laurel said, "Betcha walked here." Of course I did. And although I'm not wearing plaid, it's clear to see, from my sneakers to my jacket, I got Florence's fashion sense.

Both of them pointed out the window to a new ugly blue high-rise on the other side of Delancey. "Blue Smurf dick," they both chortled. Like I said, no bullshit.

Joyce reminded me that during those long-ago visits with Florence, they played with my long braids.

I don't remember. But sitting at Laurel's kitchen table, my Lower East Side accent returns full force and I talk like I am six again. I talk like I'm me again.

**NOT CONEY.
CONEY ISLAND.**

Florence is not only refusing to get out of bed, she is refusing visitors everything but her back.

Kay, the recreational therapist, managed to get Florence to turn to her by playing a sonatina really badly on her portable electric keyboard. Annoyed by sloppy playing, Florence rolled over, corrected Kay's mistakes, and then rolled back into her little corner.

Kay didn't give up. She began mispronouncing composers' names. Badly. Florence rolled back over and began a lesson in how one is required to speak, and how *De-buuuu-SEEE* is supposed to be pronounced.

A couple of days later, finished with my swimming lesson, which actually went swimmingly (I did not drown), I looked down from the glass balcony at the gym's pool filled with bodies going back and forth, and recalled a recent conversation with the Ex-Lover, the woman Florence had loved all her life, the woman who had loved Florence—her "Deutschie"—all her life.

They had first found each other when they were so young they still had hope, but were old enough to recognize passion and desire for one another. Decades later, they reunited, but only briefly: both too old to change their ways, or heal from a lifetime hiding from love.

A while ago I located the Ex-Lover's number and address in Florence's papers and gave her a call. To catch her up on things. As thanks, she sent me the recipe for spiced applesauce cake she got from my grandmother—the one who hated Florence. Seemed like a fair exchange

C.O. Moed

at the time.

No one knew Florence like this Ex-Lover. "Your mother, my Deutschie, was a great swimmer; your mother, my Deutschie, could swim anywhere; your mother, my Deutschie, we went to Coney and boy could your mother, my Deutschie, swim! She went out, way out, and then your mother, my Deutschie . . ."

I knew Florence and Coney went back as far as Florence and the Ex-Lover. Years ago, before we knew her memory had begun to fray and she was hiding accidents and mistakes behind closed doors, I got Florence to talk into a microphone about the place she loved more than her piano—Coney Island.

Staring at all the swimmers below me, I wondered if I could coax Florence to roll back into life.

I called her.

"Hello, Florence, I just finished another swimming lesson!"

"I used to go swimming. I swim," Florence said.

"I KNOW. IN THE OCEAN." (I had to shout this because she had—again—forgotten how to hold the phone up to her ear.)

"Right. And then you sit on the boardwalk, watch the people, and they see you alone and they try to strike up a conversation."

"Get out of bed and I'll take you to Coney."

"NOT Coney. It's Coney Island. Coney ISLAND."

"Get out of bed and I'll take you to Coney ISLAND."

"OK. Maybe tomorrow. Don't eat too much. And lie down."

And with that she clicked off to roll back into her own deep waters.

IRENE

We recognized each other immediately. No matter that we were slogging along on treadmills at the gym of an elite university, no matter that we had gone to different grade schools, no matter that we had grown up blocks away from one another in different parts of the Lower East Side, no matter that she was Chinese American, I was Jewish American. No matter. You grow up below Delancey Street, you can spot that Lower East Side moxie a mile away.

Irene still lives down there with her husband and son in the high-rise apartment buildings a block away from where Florence lives.

C.O. Moed

One rare morning we grabbed some coffee from the neighborhood luncheonette.

"It's hard for my friends to understand how it could be so fantastic to have lived a less-than-idyllic life in the Lower East Side among projects, tenements, gangs, and having to watch your back," she remarked, as we strolled down the streets we grew up on—now much nicer and safer.

It was true. Back then, everything felt real and alive and normal. Every day. Even when you were punching someone or getting punched. And when I left the neighborhood and explored the world, something was always missing. Maybe it was that moxie.

Stopping in front of one of the last remaining notions stores, we both recalled that there had been a billion stores like this one up and down Grand Street and all over Orchard.

Even though my family didn't shop in these places often—buying anything new was a rare event—I knew these old stores from tagging along with my friends and their mothers when they went shopping.

"They only look chaotic, but really they are quite organized, with all those ladders that rolled along the wall of shelves. All the hair accessories stapled outside each box. Thousands of products," Irene said. "And you have to ask for what you want. I still get my stockings there. I can't find them anywhere else."

We both peeked in. The counter people eyed us suspiciously. Ah, that familiar customer service you can only get on the Lower East Side.

"We shopped on Orchard Street every other week. Don't know what my mother was buying, but every other week," Irene continued. "The Jewish owners paid us no mind, just let us poke around and look at everything until we were ready. It wasn't like we were dressed nicely. I think it was because we were Chinese and they liked us as customers."

But things changed. A Subway sandwich shop was across the street, fancy glass apartment buildings were sticking up from behind every tenement, and a café that sold one cup of coffee for three times what our coffee cost us at the luncheonette took up the whole corner.

The old notion store was now completely out of place, a relic from long ago. A hand-written sign in the window said *No Pictures*. I don't think that stopped tourists from snapping away because the store was just so old and unusual and exotic-looking. I wanted to take a picture—not because it was so old or exotic-looking, but because I wanted to capture one last portrait of my childhood before it disappeared into thin air.

"Stand in front of the door, quick before they tell us to move," I told Irene.

She obliged, but not before checking if the coast was clear. Turning to me, she said, "I'll tell you what Orchard Street taught me. It taught me to negotiate. Those Jews didn't respect you if you didn't. If you didn't, they were insulted. These days I don't bargain. There's no one there to bargain with."

I snapped a couple more pictures real fast and then we both skedaddled before anyone complained.

"You want to know what else?" she said, "My friends and I wandered the streets incessantly. People watched out for each other. My mother never worried. When I was seven and in second grade and my brother was four, my mother walked us to the Municipal Building, we went under the turnstile and we took the 6 Lexington Train to visit my aunt in the Bronx, a cruddy part too. My mother and my father worked six days a week and sending us to spend five to seven hours in my aunt's hand laundry store—they needed the break."

To anyone else, that might sound crazy. But I knew exactly what Irene was talking about. From the time I was in grade school, I ran wild from the East River all the way to City Hall. And as little kids, my sister Louise and I walked to and from Knickerbocker Village in Chinatown on Friday nights to visit our Gramma. Walking home along Madison Street at nine o'clock at night? No big deal. It's just what you did.

Irene shook her head. "If I put my son on the 6 Train to the Bronx now, I'd be arrested."

Our coffees were done. It was time to go do housework and Florence care and get on with things. Just as we were about to say goodbye, Irene paused and then said, "Did you know everyone in our building calls your mother 'Florence, the music teacher with the fancy scarf?'"

HOW LOVELY TO BE A WOMAN

Whatever you called them—tits, titties, tatas, chest, breasts, or, as Florence called them "boosum"—the competition to grow them and buy your first training bra was fierce on Grand Street. A lot of pulling up little girl T-shirts, a lot of comparing, and a lot of despairing.

Of course, all my friends got their bras first, regardless of how big they were—and none of them were big. But their parents were not only willing to train their daughters to get used to bondage, they were willing to splurge on something completely unnecessary. Well, cheaper than a bat mitzvah or braces.

Finally, desperate to fit in and keep up, I ripped every single one of my undershirts down the middle and insisted to Florence my baby bosom had just busted out of heavy woven cotton. I actually said that: "My boosum just busted through."

You can't argue with desperate lying. Florence very reluctantly gave me ten dollars—which probably was half our food budget, knowing her—and sent me off to Grand and Orchard, where all the underwear stores, run almost exclusively by Hasid and Orthodox Jewish families, were located. No matter what store you walked in, the entire family was working there—mothers, fathers, sisters, brothers, cousins, grandparents, in-laws. Everyone.

C.O. Moed

If one of the men waited on you, he'd do this really fast you-almost-don't-see-it side-glance across your chest and then would pinpoint the exact cup size within millionths of an inch. However, if it was a woman helping you, sizing was more participatory.

Weiss Loungewear, one of the bigger stores, looked empty, so no risk running into anyone and embarrassing myself. Avoiding the men, I made a beeline straight to one of the grandmothers.

I don't even think I finished saying "A training br—" when without any warning she planted both hands on everything that I had been able to grow in twelve years. Then, just as quickly, she turned around and pulled out from the hundreds of identical thin white boxes that lined the entire wall, one specific thin white box.

A "training" brassiere appeared. She didn't even have me try it on. Just packed it up, took Florence's ten-dollar bill, and handed me a bunch of change.

Heading home, I was a bit bewildered by touch I had only experienced before from camp counselors and friends' uncles. But at least this time I was carrying proof that I was now a woman.

A couple of years ago, in need of a bra that not only really fit, but also fulfilled certain vanity criteria, I returned to one of the last remaining family-run underwear stores on Grand and Orchard.

Stepping into familiar walls stacked with hundreds of identical thin white boxes, I caught the young Hasid man at the counter giving me that you-almost-don't-see-it side-glance across my chest as I headed straight to the grandmother.

I don't even think I finished saying "underwire br—" when without any warning…

FREE RANGE KIDS

Of course, me and the couple of little girl gangs I ran with had a real playground to play in. In fact, we had three. It's just that two of them were kinda small, didn't have much stuff to play on, and were sometimes locked. And the big one was always filled with the big kids.

But it didn't matter. The whole neighborhood was our playground, and we had the run of it. Including corners like this, which in those days didn't have video surveillance because there was no such thing as video. These hidden spots became our castles and battlegrounds, our field for dodgeball and our table for jacks.

I don't ever remember *not* running around the streets of the Lower East Side. From the time I was four or five until I left for higher ground, I was out the door, rain and shine, every season there was. As long as I had finished my violin practicing and homework, the world was my oyster and my little girl gangs my posse.

C.O. Moed

Yeah, we had run-ins with bad people, both big and small. And yeah, terrible things happened. But that shit was happening at home, too. We all learned to dodge and survive. Those skills paid off when I moved "uptown" to the 1970s East Village and got new! and different! problems. Like crack addicts, idiot boyfriends, and jobs with treacherous bosses.

Today's sidewalks are not filled with kids anymore. The kids today arrange play dates and meet in homes and other nice places with adult chaperones. And the streets are filled with not-kids texting or shouting highly personal information into their cell phones.

Maybe that's less dangerous, but it is much more annoying. Dodging and surviving folks looking at their phones and not where they are walking, I wonder if they ever went, when they were four or five, outside by themselves and played in a city.

YEUDI

This is how she looks today, and it's also exactly how she looked forty years ago when we met in fifth grade.

    She was one of the new girls transferred from PS 134 on East Broadway to PS 110 on Broome Street. I heard her mother ran a newsstand at Times Square and cooked from *New York Times* recipes. That made this new girl even more exotic and worldly and exciting. Glimpsing her in the beat-up school halls, I thought she floated on beauty clouds. She was so clean and graceful and unwavering.

    I was a baby monkey on caffeine who needed a bath. I longed to have her elegant grace. I still do.

    I had my first real birthday party at her house (it was a surprise!). Together we survived the tough girls punching us by Kozy Korner on a regular basis. Together we survived the teenage boys and old men grabbing our new tits on a regular basis. Together we survived the really tough Junior High School 56 on Henry Street where we got stuck with hatpins in gym class for being bad basketball players. Together we faced math every day. And she survived Willie Joe spraying her in the face with Pledge that day in seventh grade. (Man, when she chased Willie Joe down Pitt Street, it was a fierce sight to behold.)

                        C.O. Moed

And after all that, we survived the High School of Performing Arts where the dancers and actresses ruled the boys, and us musicians (her piano, me violin) had to be inventive just to be seen (I gave up and hid in the staircase during lunch for two years).

Together we ate too much, drank too much, smoked too much. We did a lot of things too much. But we *never*, *ever* threw up on the street. At some point in our late teens, maybe early twenties, we were roommates in my first and only apartment. I have the lamp, table, and cup and bowl she left behind. I still have the IMPERIALISM SUCKS poster from the 1969 March on Washington against the Vietnam War. She still looks like she lives here when she visits.

But what I remember most and always was the day in sixth grade when we got back our creative writing assignments. I don't remember what I wrote. Given that I was a lover of Nancy Drew and Charles Addams, it was probably something not great and a bit weird. But the moment I read her piece my life changed. This, I remember thinking, *this* is real writing. *This* is literature.

ONE DAY ON THE BMT

Like the 2006 photograph of Britney Spears's labia, the woman's wallet peeked out of her jacket pocket.

I leaned over and said, "Miss, your wallet is going to get stolen."

She gave me that thank-fuck-you look, the favorite glare of all those who just moved here and think they have street cred because they've visited the neighborhood's last remaining bodega down the street from their luxury condo.

I shrugged, went back to watching the subway fly by local stops.

But inside, I cursed Florence and the day she caught me stealing a stick of penny gum from the newspaper-candy store on Delancey Street, had me apologize to the owner, and then made me promise never to steal again.

C.O. Moed

THE MEN'S PARK

This is The Men's Park. Men used to play here.

They played chess and sometimes checkers, but mostly chess, on these stone boards.

We were always told to NEVER go into The Men's Park.

So of course we did. Not a lot, but enough to feel like we were breaking rules and tempting fate.

Once there, The Men utterly ignored us as we hung around the chess table, bored out of our minds with a stupid game that didn't include punching and running really fast.

The Men weren't too thrilled either with sweaty-snotty-fidgeting-dirty kids interrupting their concentration.

I could see the canopy of trees in that park from my bedroom window.

Bigger than the rest of the trees in the playground, they were the clock of the seasons. Each day I'd stick my head out of the window, looking for that green that let me know summer was about to come back. And then, all too soon, hints of reds and oranges would start popping out, telling me summer was about to leave and the misery of school was about to begin.

C.O. Moed

THE DISCIPLES OF DISCIPLINE

really hated playing the violin. But, even more than playing, I really hated practicing the violin. Regardless, every day after school, the music stand would be set up, the etude books opened, the bow rosined, the violin tuned.

Florence would take her place in the big armchair and the torture would begin.

But at some point the room would grow dim with winter evening, and she'd begin to doze.

Perhaps she was tired from her own six hours of daily piano practicing, or perhaps it was from the daily sherry she allowed herself, but only after those six hours had been completed. I didn't care. Her snores heralded my freedom.

I'd stop mid-note and if she didn't stir with her usual order of "Commence!" I'd jump into action.

Quickly scattering the music books to make it look like I had finished not only all the scales and exercises but even the piece I was studying, I'd prop the violin rakishly in its case as if it had run a long race and was catching its breath. The finishing touch was dangling the bow from the music stand as if, too hot from ferocious playing, it needed cooling.

More often than not, at this moment, the lack of my scratching out unloved music would jar Florence into Awake. And I'd have to at least do one more etude for her. But every once in a while, she'd continue snoring and I'd actually get to sneak out of the living room and happily do anything else but practice.

Still, the next day the music stand would be set up, the etude books opened, the bow rosined, the violin tuned and, like Sisyphus and his rock, I'd have to begin all over again.

Years later, Florence asked me what I really wanted to do. I was either in the middle of yet another mind-numbing job or one of my three forays into higher education. Whatever the circumstances were, I was burnt-out, drained, and exhausted from decades of juggling early morning and late-night sessions, writing stories that insisted on being told.

I hesitated answering her because my desire seemed so outlandish. Finally, I responded: "I just want to stay home and write full-time."

She was silent, like she was listening to the sentence over and over and over again.

Then she said, "You have to train for that."

༄

Early alarm, coffee made, breakfast eaten, email glanced at, the table cleared, pens lined up, doors closed, documents opened, the writing book readied, phones put aside, tiredness banished, the world shut out, the soul called forth, the heart welcomed, the hands warmed . . .

. . . the cat given a count-down . . .
Commence!
And the writing begins.

C.O. Moed

THE SECRET OF THE FRUIT MAN

For the first time ever, the Fruit Man by the Avenue A bus stop on Clinton and Grand was closed—well, the first time that wasn't a Jewish holiday.

His fruit stand, an outside pyramid of overflowing old boxes piled onto the sidewalk and a beat-up space inside for the stuff that couldn't stand the heat or the rain or the snow, was just like all the other fruit and vegetable stands in the neighborhood. But while the rest dissolved into fancy supermarkets or gourmet coffee shops or Chinatown where fresh fruit sold out of its shipping boxes still meant something, the Fruit Man stayed on Grand Street.

Everyone in the neighborhood went to him. Even Florence, who hated him. Irene, my fellow Lower East Side girl and Florence's neighbor, loved his cantaloupe. I knew he couldn't have been evicted. The City sold the building to the tenants so that everyone could stay there without being kicked out because they weren't rich.

So I called Irene. "Where's the Fruit Man?"

"He retired," Irene said.

"Really? Why? Was he sick?"

"No. He was ninety."

"He was mean."

"No he wasn't."

"He yelled at everyone."

Irene cut me off. "All his customers were old and hard of hearing. That's why he yelled."

The Gay Pride March 1982.

Everybody came out to . . . come out.

All the other gay seniors rode. In the convertible, on the bus, in wheelchairs.

Not Florence.

Fifty-eight years old. Waited her entire life to walk down a street as who she really was. And she wasn't going to give up that walk for anybody or anything.

SNAPSHOTS FROM DEEP WATER:
THE SWEET SPOT

Curve yourself onto that soft edge between your back and your belly. Like Matisse's paintbrush pouring into a reclining woman, pour into that sweet spot and then glide toward home, home being the other side of the pool.

Or glide toward a new home that only looks like the middle of the bed.

It's the beginning of that last journey to another shore.

C.O. Moed

THE NOT-ON-TV OFFICE:
WON'T YOU BE MY NEIGHBOR?

Fish gotta swim. Birds gotta fly. Bills gotta get paid. And they call it work for a reason. The Day Job starts becoming a much-needed flexible-thirty-hours-a-week break from Florence stuff, unless I have to get on the phone with the insurance company, Medicaid, CASA II, the doctor's office, the home attendant agency, the insurance company again, the doctor's office again, CASA II again, the agency again . . .

But mostly, each day I step into my cubicle and, like part of a flotilla, I bob along with my favorite cubicle neighbors until it's time to leave.

Nick is in the cubicle on my left.

He talks to me over the "hedges."

Sometimes I hear him giggling in shock while he listens on his headphones to Wendy Williams on WBLS. We lend each other books. Because of him I'm trapped in the middle of an adolescent vampire series where I am reliving every disastrous crush I ever had—only these book characters have better luck than me, even when they want to suck the blood out of the one they love.

I lent him a book about a woman's spiritual journey. I'm not sure if that's an even exchange, especially after he confesses he reads two pages on the train and falls dead asleep.

He makes coffee every day. I supply popcorn. He's the go-to man for pop culture. I supply the moral advice.

This is Adriene. She's in the cubicle on my right.

C.O. Moed

This is what I see when we talk.

If it's not Monday we talk quite a bit.

She listens to Michael Baisden on 97KISS FM. This is an actual exchange:

A: Oh he's so nauseating.

C: Why do you listen to him?

A: Because he's an idiot.

Her radio, unlike my radio, doesn't get static. So I end up listening to her radio over the cubicle wall. Sometimes we sing together, and when Baisden plays "Rock Steady" by Aretha, I turn on my radio and hug it so it doesn't get static, and then me and Adriene chair-dance in stereo.

She's the go-to woman for basic information, like the seizures-and-video-game connection, best methods to kill mice, and the '70s. I supply the cheerful morning greetings, and one day even a home-baked gluten-free loaf of bread, which turned out to be inedible to both humans and mice.

When she really wants to upset me she offers to hug me. When I really want to upset her I talk about foods with wheat.

One late night, the office empty and quiet, I get on the phone and once again attempt to coax Florence into doing something . . . like live again. Even with Gabriella, the Medicaid Monday-through-Wednesday home attendant, holding the phone for her, it's hopeless and, finally in defeat, I end up saying how much I love her and I'll see her soon, before hanging up.

Knocked down seven.

Out of nowhere, I hear Adriene: "You're a good daughter."

Get up eight.

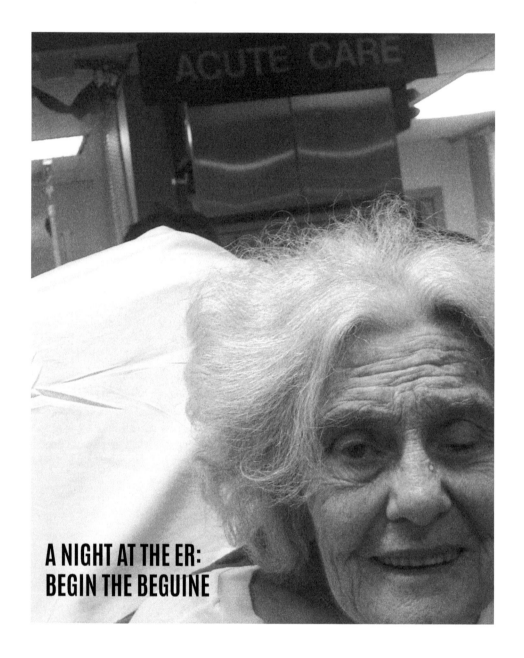

A NIGHT AT THE ER:
BEGIN THE BEGUINE

The Job is on the BMT line, express stop. So I beat the ambulance to the ER. Because when the MTA works, it works. Even at evening rush hour.

Penny, the Thursday-through-Sunday Medicaid home attendant, jumps out and shrugs, "She's fine. Cursed me all the way up." We both knew Florence was OK, but good to do it by the book.

I do my "look in eyes, shake hands" with both ambulance drivers, just in case we run into them again. They recount the various comments Florence made on the way up. Judging from their attempts at diplomacy, it is clear she's not their usual pick-up-sick-old-lady run.

The ER is packed with a lot of old people ranging from normal old sick stuff to normal old dying stuff. We get parked in a corridor. Penny splits back to the apartment. Good time to catch up on the incontinence-laundry pile.

Hospital Rule Number One: with an old person who spent the last month in bed refusing to do anything except pretend to sleep while listening to the radio, do everything you can to keep their clothes on, no matter what hospital personnel request. Because you know once those sweatpants come off Florence, it will be impossible to get them back on Florence.

So Just Say No.

Say, "Pull up her shirt and hook her up to the EKG that way."

Say, "You don't need her in a gown for the X-ray because doesn't it just go through the clothes?"

Say, "She is not being checked into the hospital. I'm in charge of my mother's care. We are going home, so I'm not putting her in a gown."

Don't say that last one out loud. Yet. But be prepared to say it a hundred times later.

The X-ray technician asks, "Are you related?"

"Daughter."

"That's related."

Because I rarely call Florence "Mom" I'm often mistaken for the home aide.

A couple of hours later, we're moved to a better and much less drafty part of the corridor because all the stalls are still packed.

A whole bunch of cops and firefighters wheel in a crazy old man, a nostalgic reminder of the 1980s when Reagan cut funding and the mentally ill poured onto the streets the next day to become the new homeless. He is handcuffed to the wheelchair. As he passes us, it sounds like he is screaming "Stupid spirit!" which I think is a pretty imaginative curse. One of the women cops corrects me: "Stupid fill-in-any-ethnicity-you-want . . ." We listen to him scream for the next hour the following:

"You fucking Nazi."

"You fucking Spic."

"Why am I handcuffed?"

"Get these fucking handcuffs off me."

"Nazi, Nazi, Nazi, Nazi hospital. I didn't want to come here."

In between the screaming, Mr. Nurse C tries to draw Florence's blood. But people keep going back and forth with stretchers. So he has to step out of the way a lot. He doesn't get much. I sing numbers from Sondheim musicals to Florence as he takes another stab at it.

"Door Rings! Phone Chimes! In Comes Companeeee!"

"NO! THAT'S WRONG!!" Florence yells. "IT'S PHONE CHIMES! DOOR RINGS . . . OWWWW!!" Mr. Nurse C's finally got a good vein.

The screaming old man quiets down—either he got moved or he got sedated. The firefighters and the cops head out. The really cute firefighter says to the other really cute firefighter, "What do I know? I'm just a stupid Spic." The woman cop complains to her partner, "I don't wanna leave my handcuffs here."

A doctor suddenly appears at our gurney with all of Florence's paperwork. He's young, good-looking and got that small-butch-in-command mojo swagger going on. If he had a soundtrack it would be the Commodores' "Too Hot ta Trot," he is so delicious.

Dr. Hot-ta-Trot asks Florence, "Are you home?"

Florence looks up at him and says, "Well, I'll call it home."

I have been holding her hand during everything. My nose itches. I scratch it and smell her urine. Find a hand-sanitizer dispenser and clean both of our hands.

"Have you ever taken care of anyone like this before?" Florence asks me.

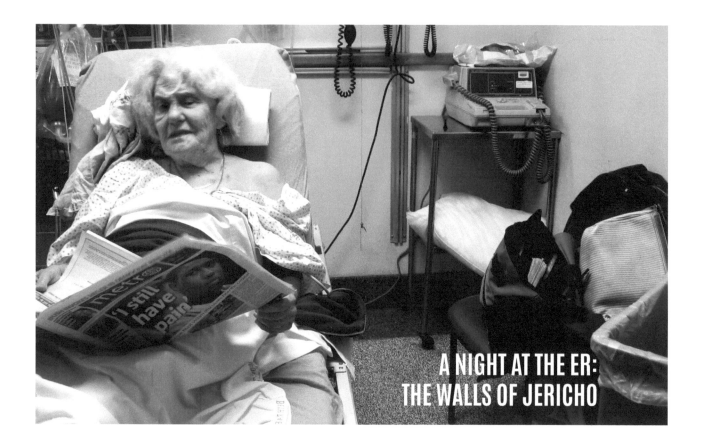

A NIGHT AT THE ER:
THE WALLS OF JERICHO

Many, many hours later we finally get a stall. And I begin: "She is not being checked into the hospital I'm in charge of my mother's care we are going home so I'm not putting her in a gown she is not being checked into the hospital I'm in charge of my mother's care we are going home so I'm not putting her in a gown she is not being checked into the hospital I'm in charge of my mother's care we are going home so I'm not putting her in a gown . . ."

Even when the supervisor of *Dr. Hot-ta-Trot* warns me that they can't be responsible if I refuse to do what they say I should do, which really means if something goes wrong with your mother we're going to make sure you go to jail.

I've heard it all before. I also know if she stays in the hospital, things will go more downhill than they already have, and right now things are so downhill we're digging a tunnel.

All the tests come back fine—her heart, her lungs, her pressure, her blood. I do not say "told you!" I just pretend to look relieved.

Dr. Hot-ta-Trot then wonders maybe she has a urinary tract infection. "Can you get her to pee? If not, we can easily catheterize her." He seems very excited about that.

Questions that separate the men from the boys:

     How many times have you seen your mother's vagina and urethra and asshole?

     How intimate are you with the smells of those places you now wipe clean on a regular basis?

     How often do you make decisions about those places?

C.O. Moed

"No catheters. It will be too upsetting. Let's try the bedpan."

And with that, I agree that Florence's clothes can come off. But We.Are.Not.Admitting.Her.Overnight.

You gotta draw the line somewhere.

For a frail old lady, Florence has dense, heavy bones to move. It takes the new night nurse, Ms. Nurse D, and me ten minutes to pull off the sweatpants and slip the metal bedpan under her. An hour later a hopeful check only finds the empty pan suctioned tight to Florence's bottom. In between her shouting "Ow ow ow that hurts," Ms. Nurse D and I pry the bedpan off her shrunken butt and a small plastic one is quickly slipped under her instead.

Then we shove as many little apple juice boxes as we can into her hands and she slurps away happily. Soon she is sleeping.

Dr. Hot-ta-Trot pops his head into the stall. "Anything?!" Man, this guy is so excited about the possibility of pee. "Don't worry! It will happen!" His shift ends in a few minutes and what he really wants is to find out if his hunch was right.

Suddenly, things get quiet and empty.

As if New York decided to take a break from car accidents and deranged homeless people and sidewalk falls and life-threatening illness.

And suddenly I am tired. About to hit fifty, heartbroken, and exhausted from being Shirley Temple—always marching along with a chirpy little song and a happy little tap—before I can stop myself I start crying.

Out of nowhere, I hear Florence's voice. "Laughing or crying?"

I look up. She is completely alert and sharp and curious.

"Crying."

"I want you to feel better," she states. "I had to change in later years. Working."

I sit up. "Working? Like teaching piano working?"

"No," she says. "Working on myself. Becoming equal to what I had wanted to do." And then she looks at me . . . she looks at me and . . .

A few hours ago she didn't know my name or that I was her daughter. I was just the person she knew would take care of her, rub her back, sing her songs, help her feel better—love her like a mommy loves her little girl.

But suddenly, in this quiet and empty ER, after fifty years of me knocking on closed doors, waiting patiently under the grand piano and walking silently next to her as she stomped through the city battling her demons, someone else is looking at me.

And although I only met her a couple of times in my life, I'd recognize her anywhere.

For here, in a stall with plastic curtains drawn around us like a shawl, from the midst of her disintegrating into wisps of childlike desperate need, I suddenly see my mother again.

"I'm going to give you a drink!" she declares.

"Of what? Scotch?" It was what we drank together at an old bar in the East Village, never mind that I was still underage.

"No!" We are now both grinning at each other.

Out of nowhere a herd of doctors stomp into the next stall and wake up the addict there.

"We're going to give you Narcan."

"No! No! I don't want Narcan."

"Well did you take anything?"

"NO! NO! I just fell asleep on the bench."

"Then why won't you take Narcan?"

"No! No!"

Florence and I look at each other like *wow*. What was that?

We rest. I can't take my eyes off of her and she keeps looking at me.

She finally says, "Is there anything I can give you?"

"You're giving me something right now. You're listening to me."

"Well," she says with strength from decades ago, "I'm listening!"

I say, "I think this was one of our best visits ever."

But she dismisses me. "Oh, I like the other one where you put all the . . .

"Music?"

"Yeah."

And I hear myself speak like the daughter I never got to be. "I'm just sad."

"When you say the word 'sad,' I can feel it. You always say you're OK. Makes me think it's . . ." Another word gone.

"A facade?"

"Yeah."

"I am OK. But I'm sad."

"Why don't you go to a shrink? Get a minor . . ."

"What? Key?"

Shakes head.

"Start changing. Start changing the change of the different changes of the . . ."

I lean in, hoping my body acts like magnet for her words but she is fading.

". . . and then start out with what you have with starting with a different . . ."

"What? Job? Attitude? Approach?"

"No. What I can think of it . . . that way is better . . ."

And then she starts to count.

"One-two-three. Four-five-six. One-two-three. Four-five-six."

We look at each other.

"A different time signature?" I ask.

"Yeah."

My childhood as her pupil, spent learning notes and keys and rhythms.

And time signatures. The beats between two bars. The measure of each note. The pulse within the walls of a home.

My cousin once told me it was not the trumpets that brought down the walls of Jericho. It was the tears of the women.

I weep. Out loud. And I weep out loud, not from a broken heart, but from a heart that has broken open.

"You look awful," Florence says.

The addict, furious at the treatment he was offered but refused to take because it didn't include the pain killers he wanted, screams at the doctor who has told him to leave the ER, "I HOPE YOUR CHILDREN ARE ALL FAGGOTS AND THEY DIE OF AIDS."

C.O. Moed

A NIGHT AT THE ER: THE ELEVENTH HOUR

t is now eleven hours since we arrived at the ER. Ms. Nurse D comes in and we find that all the apple juice we plied Florence with was happily peed out—not into the little plastic tub, but all over the sheets, the pads, the blanket, the bed. There is nothing left to do but catheterize her.

I hold Florence's hand and sing her numbers from Sondheim musicals.

Somehow there's still some pee left inside her and the filled plastic bag is whisked away and we all find out she has a urinary tract infection, which is one reason she couldn't get out of bed for the last couple of months.

A prescription is called in to the twenty-four-hour pharmacy, a private ambulance is summoned to take us home, and two Amazons, with no effort whatsoever, move Florence from bed to stretcher and whoosh her into the ambulance.

I quickly kill the roach running around the back, but Florence somehow sees it. "Was that a roach?!"

At 10:50 p.m. we finally roll into her home lobby. Now all we have to do is get Florence from the stretcher to the wheelchair.

One of the Amazons scoops Florence into her arms. Florence, utterly befuddled, stares up at the Amazon in childlike wonder. Without thinking I blurt out, "Florence! It's your dream come true! You're in the arms of a beautiful woman."

And with that she is gently plopped into the wheelchair.

We can't all fit in the tiny elevator. "They are going to take you up in the elevator and I'm going to take the stairs and meet you up on the fifth floor."

Florence's face crumbles. "But I want to go with you . . ."

Both Amazons go "AAAAWWWWWWW . . ."

I run up five flights of stairs, and all four of us—the two Amazons, Penny who has waited up for us, and me—manage to get Florence out of sheets and wheelchair and confusion to face her bed.

When Florence sees it for the first time, her face lights up like a child opening a present. "OH!"

The other Amazon scoops up Florence in her arms like a prince to a princess or a lover to a lover. Or a really strong woman to a frail old lady. She gently places Florence in bed. Penny and I cover her up.

Florence is finally home.

But the mother who wanted to buy me a drink is gone and I haven't seen her since.

I head out to the twenty-four-hour pharmacy.

BEAUTY IN THE EYE OF . . .

Any bar that's a real bar has her over the cash register. No matter what neighborhood the bar is in, she's there.

This East Village bar that smells of cat pee and dead rats has had her there since the 1970s, and I'm sure my cigarette smoke is part of the layer of grime that coats her.

I don't know if she has a name, or if each bar names her themselves. I just know that at 12:09 at night—or in the morning if you're really going to be a dick about it—sitting at the bar by myself and recapturing the weekend's highs and lows of perseverance and loneliness, I find it reassuring to see a voluptuous woman command such respect and radiate such beauty.

THE RIGHT TO GLITTER AND BE GAY

I don't think I was the only one to take Florence to a dyke bar. But I know I was the only one who took her to one on her sixtieth birthday.

We huddled at the bar and I know we drank because I never knew Florence to not drink when there was something available to drink.

I pulled out a pile of wrapped presents—all books—and said "Happy birthday."

Each and every one of those books was about getting older in Lesbianland—coming out, getting freed, living your life on your own terms.

We looked through them and drank and looked some more and drank some more and then I think she went off to meet friends. (I was not invited. That's because she didn't tell her gal pals she had kids. Boy, were they surprised at her memorial.)

It was the 1980s and the world outside the bars wasn't safe for old girls, especially gay ones. Sure, Florence fought with and chased after more than a couple of muggers. But she also lived in a neighborhood that watched everything she did, suspected what she was, and judged what she wanted. And what she wanted and what she was was still considered a mental illness, even if the American Psychiatric Association had taken it off the sicko list.

But that bar? That bar was safe. That bar and all the bars like it gave shelter from the storm.

Florence took her books back home, and in between teaching piano students in her living room she'd pull them out from under the couch and look at the life she was finally calling her own.

I don't know if she ever hung out at that bar again. I just know it was there if she wanted to. Whatever she did or didn't do, that night we both felt safe from the world and got to celebrate her birth, her day, and her life as who and what she was, and toast what she wanted for her new year.

II ANDANTE
CON MOTO

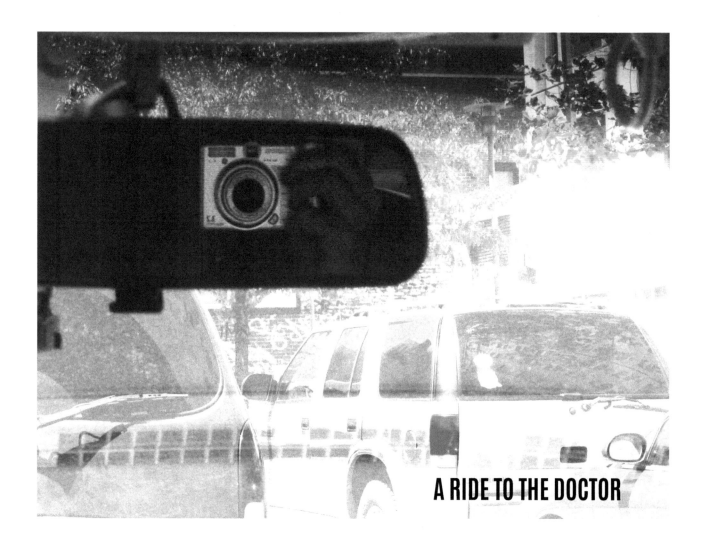

A RIDE TO THE DOCTOR

The day was bright. There was something clean and crisp in the air. Not spring. February.

On any kind of day, it takes an army to get an old person who can't walk or breathe normally to the corner of Broome and Columbia where the Delancey Car Service waits.

The dispatcher only gives you three minutes to get to the corner. And when you get there the driver insists you were told one minute. Still, on this day the driver waited; sunny, clear days that are not too cold are slow. All the old people who can walk without assistance take the Avenue A bus.

I greeted this guy with the smile I greet everyone and anyone with who I have to enlist to help me take care of Florence. It says: *Isn't she cute this little old lady practically toppling over and dying in my arms and I'm only three inches taller than her but clearly I'm her daughter just look at the cheekbones and we even dress alike—parka, beret, sneakers—right? and look how much I'm caring for my old mother aren't we a sympathetic sight?*

C.O. Moed

And, like the car service guys before him, this one smiled back and lightened up about us taking more than three minutes to get to the corner. That gave me hope he would be good-natured about waiting at the Curb of Insanity at Beth Israel's outpatient facility while I dodged a billion other car services and Access-A-Ride vans to run in and find a wheelchair to bring out to the car.

The car zipped onto Delancey. I had about fifteen minutes of not panicking before we got to the Curb of Insanity. At the red light, Florence read aloud all the signs in the window of the last remaining Spanish-Chinese restaurant in the city. "Apollo. Restaurant. Lunch Specials. $8.95. That's expensive."

Light changed and we watched the new-stores-eating-up-all-the-old-stores fly by. Turning up First Avenue, the street looked as it does on an empty Sunday: a wide boulevard of another city, maybe in Europe—stately and gracious, the buildings suddenly with character, not tarted-up tenements with $2,000-a-month rent for a studio.

"The day is beautiful," Florence murmured.

"Yeah," I said. "Look at those trees."

"I'm not interested in nature!" she snapped.

UPSTAIRS, DOWNSTAIRS

Florence worked at Grossinger's when the Catskills were the posh place to be. That's her on the left side with her chin in her hand.

Grossinger's was kosher; that meant you didn't mix meat with milk. There was a story of Florence almost getting fired for bringing a glass of milk to a little girl in the meat dining room. In another version, Mr. Grossinger himself chased her around the kitchen with a knife.

She told me she once gave a New York taxi driver making a drop-off at the resort all her cash tips to bring down to her mother back on Hester Street. Needless to say, it never got there.

She may have also worked at the Youngs Gap Hotel in Parksville and the Flagler in South Fallsburg. Flagler's postcard says it's a country club with a golf course and wooded trails to ride horses on. I didn't meet people who rode horses until I was a teenager hanging around a rich New Age commune. I didn't meet anyone who played golf until I was almost thirty.

Working at these places Florence wore the starched white collar, black dress of a waitress, not a pianist. Did any of the people she served see her?

Did any of them know that, despite the dishonest cabdriver, she was able to save up enough cash from all her waitressing jobs to purchase her own Steinway?

Did any of them know her playing would one day be described as brilliant, presented in a vivid color and compelling rhythmic force, or that her Chopin demonstrated an affinity with the composer?

She never, to my knowledge, ever got to stay in places like this.

C.O. Moed

FROM THAT MOMENT ON, LIFE WAS DIFFERENT

Sheynah Meydeleh told us.

Of course none of us believed her. But she insisted. She had it on good authority and could even prove it to us.

So we all trooped off to the children's section of the Seward Park Library on East Broadway where the librarian nodded gravely at Sheynah Meydeleh's request and then guided us to a little bookcase we had never really paid attention to before. There she pulled out a big-enough picture book with big-enough pictures called *How Babies Are Made*.

The sudden information that not only did our fathers have one of those, but also that they did that with our mothers left us numb and shocked.

That is, until we discovered dirty jokes.

THE NOT-ON-TV-OFFICE: ANNIE'S SONG

A nnie and I work together. Don't know how, but one day we realized we both came from the Lower East Side. Same block, but a much different street.

She talks faster than I write, and I write faster than I talk and I talk fast. So some of this she said and some of this I hope she said:

> We lived on East 138th Street. My mom, aunt, my uncle on the weekend. Eight of us kids. Then we moved to East Tenth.
>
> And then we moved to Grand Street, across from the bialy place and the delicatessen. And then we moved down the street to Pitt and Grand. Nine of us, two rooms, we all slept in the same beds together. We were right across from the co-ops, which was the forbidden land.

THIS IS ANNIE AS A SONG

C.O. Moed

Tenements, you had the poorer people. You knew you didn't belong in the co-ops, but they knew they didn't belong with us. We played together sometimes, but there was this line down the middle of the street. A yellow line that divided us. They still thought less of you. And the special buildings they put up for the bar mitzvahs. This was before they did bat mitzvahs. Huge tents.

We lived on the top floor and Rosy's Pizza and Heroes was on the ground floor. We would line up and she would give us free fried dough in sauce. We couldn't afford the sandwiches.

The old principal at PS 134—Jewish woman, red hair, dressed like Joan Rivers, eyelashes, bangles up her arm—and all she had to do was look at you. Then we had an African American teacher—female. Wore miniskirts, blue eye shadow, overweight—fourth or fifth grade? First one to introduce us to Africa. Because of Biafra. We brought in pennies to donate. We thought we had it bad. We didn't have it that bad. 1966? 1967?

The principal, Miss Cohen? She was ahead of her time. But miniskirts. That teacher used to wear miniskirts. It's the life we knew but it's gone. A sense of community. Gone.

And you can't forget the egg creams.

Laurel and Joyce's Uncle Joe and my Uncle George were friends. This was taken at the Wittmyers Picture Studio on Rivington Street.

They both played the trombone. Uncle George was born with three fingers and a thumb and you could play trombone if that's all you had.

They were pretty good, played in school orchestras and even in the City Amateur Orchestra at Prospect Park in 1942.

But after the war both of them left New York and that was that. The only thing Uncle Joe wanted from New York was his trombone. His mother mailed it to him. Uncle George's oldest daughter has his trombone. She's talking about playing it one day.

Meanwhile we got the photos that tell us our families' stories.

Not so much in the rest of the neighborhood. When the old people die in the old neighborhood, usually it's their kids who clean out the apartment. So they know what to keep.

But sometimes their kids send their kids who don't know what's what. And sometimes there are no kids so it's the niece or the nephew or their kids.

And sometimes it's not even family. Sometimes it's the kids of the neighbors next door—complete strangers—who clean out the life of a person who had no one to call their own except the people in photos left behind.

THE GIRLS NEXT DOOR AND THEIR PHOTO ALBUM

Which is how Laurel found all these old photos tossed in the garbage. She rescued them so that a discarded life and history could always have a home.

Did Herman ever make it here or did he die there, maybe in a pogrom or in the camps? Or maybe, just maybe he grew to be the soldier

This is the Delancey Street Florence roamed. The Delancey Loews theater in the background still looked like that when we went there on Saturday afternoons.

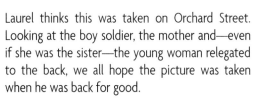

Laurel thinks this was taken on Orchard Street. Looking at the boy soldier, the mother and—even if she was the sister—the young woman relegated to the back, we all hope the picture was taken when he was back for good.

On the back of this, in beautiful fountain pen cursive, someone wrote "Herman. He played for the Czar." Since the only Russians who came to America in the early 1900s were Jews, all we could think was this was a Jew who played for the Czar. That was a big, big deal.

in that other picture and maybe, just maybe that soldier came back alive.

Me, Laurel, and Joyce looked at this guy and we all said, "He looks familiar. That place looks familiar."

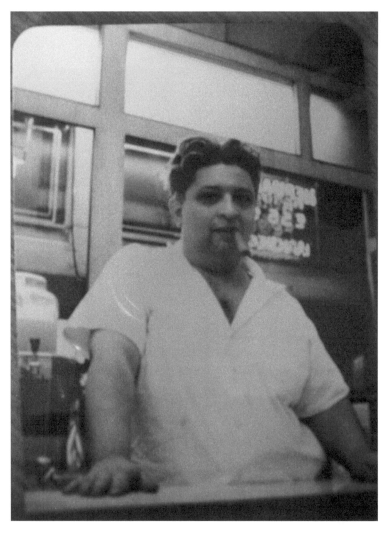

This picture, every inch of it, is proof of those rare delicious moments I had as a kid—the evening dark, the clock early, the smells of an overused luncheonette grill mingling with burnt coffee and cigarette and cigar smoke, and the traffic noise from the bridge music.

And maybe the rare treat of a five-cent seltzer with a two-cent pretzel.

THE BUREAU OF BUBBLE GUM

There was no avoiding shots, so there was no avoiding Dr. Goldfarb's office, which was on Lewis Street. It was on the ground floor of the building my parents had lived in when they began making a family, up the street from PS 110 where we went to school, across the street from Kozy Korner where I got punched a lot and also where I coveted the too-expensive Poor Little Rich Boy, Archie-Veronica, and Superman comic books.

The unbearableness of being stuck with thick, heavy needles was only mitigated by a small bowl on Dr. Goldfarb's desk, filled to the top with Bazooka Bubble Gum.

For two little girls whose parents refused them sweets and candies and sodas and cakes except at Gramma's house on Friday nights, that piece of gum was the Holy Grail we could claim by journeying through the hell of vaccinations.

The small pink rectangle with its magical smell of something delicious, the literary merits of the cartoon, the repeating of the joke on the bottom, the many methods of the first bite, either breaking it along the middle line, or popping all of it into the mouth or nibbling the edges or . . .

Doctor visits only happened once or twice a year, and that gum had to last a little bit longer than one day. So my sister and I were allowed to stick our gum on the side of our bureaus, and each day after school we would get to have that piece of bubble gum once again.

Within days, the gum would become unchewable. And so the wait for the next shot would begin.

HEAVY LIFTING: LATANYA

In the scramble of putting care around Florence, we met LaTanya. She was one of those chair-next-to-bed companions from the hospital. And she was completely unfazed by anything Florence said. That's because she looked at people the way Florence did—with curiosity and insightfulness. She was fucking smart, too, and, I found out later, a writer and a voracious reader. She was also pretty damn comfortable in the company of women like Florence. She looked at Florence and saw all of her.

She was available a couple of nights into the mornings, and with another home attendant and me taking two days since I worked part-time, and Louise doing one day—Florence suddenly had twenty-four-hour care at home.

But Florence, thrilled to be out of the hospital, assumed she was returning to her home and her life, not an apartment with strange people in it making sure she went to the bathroom alright. Lying in bed, her house keys clenched in her fist, she spent days screaming at us to "GET THESE PEOPLE OUT OF MY HOUSE!"

But it was too late. Stories were trickling in from the neighborhood and we were finding out about the too many things that had gone wrong behind our backs. We couldn't risk another fall, another burnt pot, another bathroom accident in public. Someone now had to be there.

"Do you know the word *autonomy*?" Florence barked at LaTanya. "SELF-GOVERNING!"

LaTanya told me later, "Nobody wants to clean someone's behind. The work is boring, you don't use your skills, and you're indoors. But you help people from their perspective."

So she did.

LaTanya

She was still pretty independent. I just made sure she was OK. She went to the bathroom by herself and I cooked for her. Well, tried.

But mostly I was just there to make sure she was OK. One time something went wrong in the bathroom. Feces on the wall and I knew she wasn't clean and there had been a problem. But I also knew I couldn't order her around. So I cleaned up the bathroom and then mentioned, like, "there might be something wrong" and "maybe could we check" and basically I manipulated her into the bathroom and cleaned her up.

Florence always got up earlier than me but one night—middle of the night—I heard her shuffling around. I came into her room and she was on her hands and knees looking for something under the bed and I was like "Florence, are you OK?" and she would not turn to look at me, just "No, no, no, go away."

So I stepped back, but asked again, "Let me help you." She kept waving me away trying to find something under the bed. About ten minutes later I heard "DAMMIT! IT'S NOT THERE!"

I went back in and looked under the bed and there it was—her glass eye.

I gave it to her like nothing was unusual and walked away. I told you and Louise. And you both were like, "Oh yeah, she has a glass eye." After that I would check every night to make sure it was in the eyecup.

I was going to the Borough of Manhattan Community College and I'd read her my papers. And she just let it fly: "You think you can get by without hard working? You can't. Just who do you think you are?" She checked me a lot.

And we talked a lot about correct speech. She made me repeat "asking" over and over again. "Ask-king" twenty times. She told me if you pronounce things wrong they will know your demographic. But if you speak correctly, they don't. She looked at me like I was a whole person. She saw me as a whole person.

She was still playing the piano and she was still teaching. Students were still coming by. That's long-term memory. Dementia patients have that. So she could still teach. You guys didn't realize that. When I told you, you had to call the students and tell them not to come.

But every day she still played the piano. For hours. She would be in the living room playing and I would lie down in the hallways and listen for hours. Just lie there.

I know who Bach is because of her, and one time I was in the subway and this violinist was playing Bach and I said I know that piece. It's Bach. And he looked at me like how do you know who Bach is, like I don't look like someone who knows Bach.

But I do.

Hours. Lying on the floor in the hallway by the door of the living room listening to Florence play the piano.

"Autonomy". That's a big word.

**THE NOT-ON-TV OFFICE:
THE SIX O'CLOCK NEWS AT FIVE**

A shout went up in the office: "A second guy is climbing the *New York Times* Building. They just shut down Eighth Avenue!"

So we all rushed out to look. And just like when we were kids, checking out an accident or a fire or a fistfight, we all hung out smack in the middle of the street watching the flashing lights and reenacting the news we were going to see on TV later on.

C.O. Moed

SUNDAY IN THE PARK WITH FLORENCE

As soon as I could walk on my own, I lived in the playground tucked underneath the Williamsburg Bridge. Spent every day running around by myself or with the other kids who were also regulars. When it was time for me to come home, Florence would stick her head out the window from our fifth floor apartment and call for me.

The seesaw and I had a very special relationship. I got a black eye from attempting to balance on it. And as soon as my eye healed, I tackled that son-of-a-bitch again. And got another black eye.

Then I hit thirteen and discovered boys and Washington Square Park.

Decades later, I'd pass the old playground on my way to Florence's, but never went in. At some point it got "renovated." They tore down the kindergarten building with the public bathrooms and put up a jungle gym instead. The baby swings were still there and so was the sprinkler. But the sandbox was done away with because sand was now deemed unsanitary. The seesaws and the big swings were also gone because they were now deemed too dangerous. The Bridge got painted pretty colors and was cleaned up for people who assumed they wouldn't get mugged up there, and The Men's Park stayed empty and unused.

Then Florence got sick.

The woman who could rush through her city and her life in that ferocious stride of hers—nothing stopping her, walking for miles and hours to save carfare so she could blow it on the new special at Wendy's—could barely walk further than the corner of Broome Street to get the car service to the doctor's office.

One day, during my usual offerings to take her for a walk—because what the hell, why not—suddenly she said yes. She wanted to go for a walk. Maybe to one of the "new" park benches in the shadow of the Bridge facing the sprinkler. Thrilled, I bundled her up and, with her gripping my arm, we headed out.

What used to be a five-minute stroll now took about twenty minutes.

Once there, we sat and listened to the Bridge—the only thing that hadn't changed in either of our lives. That's the thing about music the city makes—you hear it and suddenly you are fierce and young and strong and able-bodied.

I could have sat there all day, so happy Florence wasn't curled up in a fog on her bed. But she seemed to get sadder and quieter. After a while, she asked to go home.

Gripping my arm, she made her way back to the apartment—both of us not saying anything. But now there was a feeling between us, a growing awareness—this was it for her day, her world, her life. This was it.

C.O. Moed

GET OUTTA TOWN

Except for the rare trip on the Greyhound Bus to visit aunts, uncles, and cousins in Philadelphia, and later, after a purchase of a car, two trips to Atlantic City, leaving New York happened on public transportation: the F Train to Coney Island or the Staten Island Ferry to . . . well . . . nowhere really. All we did was get off the ferry, run around the corner and reenter the terminal to go back to recognizable land.

Later, when I had my own set of wheels—a three-speed Raleigh bike—or enough carfare to take the Madison Street bus to the First Avenue bus connection in Chinatown, that ferry ride became respite, refuge, and freedom. I'd stand in the back of the boat as it slugged it out with the water and learn perspective. I lived in the most beautiful city in the world, on the most beautiful harbor in the world, and I was going to be OK. Everything was going to be OK.

WHAT WE DID ON OUR NIGHT OFF

The fake purple flowers, the soft gray tones, the rose accent pillows, the comfortable couches, a lovely meeting room, big flat screens, expensive stackable chairs, the best fluorescent lights money and funding can buy . . .

It's the Alzheimer Chapter's Tuesday night "How to Bathe Your Batty Mother-Father-Husband-Wife-Aunt-Sister" workshop! How to bathe them without them freaking out, screaming, crying, wailing, and punching the shit out of you.

The workshop facilitators start the workshop with a video. I never saw anyone like my mother before, but here she is on screen, appearing as a frightened and bewildered ancient skinny bald white guy with bony sticks for legs, a not-as-ancient-but-pretty-old Black woman who is very Christian judging from the prayers she is crying out, and a middle-aged plump blonde with a southern accent clutching a dolly, begging to be left alone.

I see and hear Florence in their crying and screaming and flying fists and shouted fears, yelling they are being hurt and it's cold and it's wet and they don't want to fall and . . .

C.O. Moed

I look around. The room is packed with lots of people who have suddenly found themselves not in the relationship they started out in years before. The faces are fierce and tired, and the questions loaded and desperate.

"I took him on an expensive cruise but he wouldn't shave. Should I try to shave him?"

"Why did he stop playing the piano?"

"She is hiding soiled underwear and . . ."

"He lies about bathing but won't let anyone in the bathroom with him."

We are all clutching the remnants of someone as they slip through our fingers and plummet into insanity that only comes when something inside the head starts eating the brain for breakfast, lunch, and dinner.

"Lower your standards," the facilitators tell us.

Florence, once crisp in her chic pants she got for two dollars at the flea market at Coney Island, a bit of silk flare around her neck, a jaunty man's jacket that was more dashing than anything Katherine Hepburn ever wore, her old Stride-Rite snappy heels . . . now she's in diapers and cheap ten-dollar sweatpants that pill after only one wash.

I turn to the wall and bury myself in my workshop notes so no one sees me cry.

After tonight there will be no more baths. The baby wipes will do just fine.

TAXI

It was late. It was raining. There were no buses in sight.

I slowly raised my arm at the sea of yellow cabs barreling down Fifth Avenue, and immediately heard Florence's voice in my head yelling at me that WE.DON'T.TAKE.TAXIS. START.WALKING.

I told her to SHUT.UP. Then I got in the first one that pulled over.

He talked as fast as he drove. He drove fast.

And as we flew downtown, the history of New York and the art of bowling unfolded through stories of his family and his passion and pride for being one of the best amateurs with nineteen consecutive strikes one late night up in the Bronx.

Florence would have appreciated that.

WHEN US THREE WENT A-TRAVELING

Getting to my sister's violin teacher required serious travel. The Avenue D bus to First Avenue, and then the First Avenue bus all the way up until we landed in the land of Oz, only without the cute people singing.

The sidewalks looked like they were waiting for Fred and Ginger to dance on them—shiny and new. The building had a doorman who was better dressed than our father or, for that matter, any of the fathers we knew. And he announced us on a phone instead of hollering up from the street.

There was a restraint—a kind of silence even when they were talking—that everyone wore like corsets. It was bewildering to me. Like stepping into a frozen cartoon from Florence's *New Yorker* magazine and not understanding a word anyone said.

What I did understand was Florence's posture suddenly becoming regal, and her unspoken admonishment to be on our best behavior.

This was uptown.

WHEREVER YOU ARE THERE YOU ARE

"**W**here are you?" Florence would demand as she sat in that beat-up old black chair watching *Singing in the Rain* or *Sister Act* again. I'd usually be sitting next to her, knitting, jotting notes, taking a picture.

Her hand would skitter out from under the chair blanket and, never taking her eyes off the screen of a movie she couldn't remember having seen a week earlier, find my hand and grab it tight.

I'd stop knitting, jotting, snapping, and the two of us would watch the movie I did remember seeing over and over and over again. And the tap dancing would tap and the singing would sing and the rain would rain and the nuns would nun and the trains outside would go by and Sunday afternoon would pass.

And then one day, she didn't care where I was. That's because Joni, my long-ago ex-girlfriend, was visiting.

Florence loved Joni, and when I told her we were breaking up and Joni was going back to California, she punched me really hard. Joni loved that about Florence. "Nice to have her on my side," she remarked later.

Somehow Joni and I managed to remain close. And when she came back to her New York home, she always visited Florence. Bountiful conversations would pour out about art and paint and notes and light and the *New York Times*.

C.O. Moed

But now, there was less of Florence to visit with.

Still, Joni came by this Sunday afternoon. Florence was thrilled to see her. Sat grinning in her chair, but couldn't make a full sentence into a full idea.

Finally, like a kid showing a guest her most precious belonging, Florence said she wanted to show her this great movie. "*Singing in the Rain*! Have you seen it?!"

It didn't matter Joni had seen it with Florence many years ago. She got comfortable and I turned the movie on yet again.

We were all there.

THE DAY

It's Sunday, and I've arrived with my usual bags of food from various eating joints. Penny has successfully cleaned Florence up and gotten her to the kitchen table.

The *ALL THE JAZZ YOU CAN EAT* show is on, and Sinatra pours out of the old kitchen table radio. Florence sings along furiously, and at some point to hell with Sinatra wherever he is in the song, she is in the middle of her own rendition. She motions me to join in, and I sing along with her as I dish food onto her plate.

"I am singing every note in tune! You don't sing in tune!" Florence yells at me.

I don't bother to argue with her that she is in a different key than the radio. Like most recent experiences, it really doesn't matter. All that matters is that right now Florence needs me to be incapable of singing as well as she does, keys be damned. It's the highlight of her week.

Coleslaw shakes precariously on her fork. I hover with a napkin. Florence hates everything she eats, save the coleslaw. That she'll eat without telling me how awful it tastes.

I cut another piece of meatloaf. Hand it to her. Do the mommy thing of "Just one bite. Come on, you need to eat some more . . ."

She bites. "This is terrible."

It's the third sandwich I've tried on her this week. Nothing works. "How can I make it better?"

"Make the food taste good again."

I stare at all the pills I've poured into little neat daily piles. The drugs keeping her alive are killing her life.

C.O. Moed

A PARALLEL UNIVERSE IN THE ELEVATOR

I needed a break from worrying and calling and emailing and strategizing (Is the eye infected can we get her out of bed did the insurance company/Medicaid/doctor's office get the fax can we let her make decisions so she feels it's still her life what about the air conditioner what if I go up to the insurance company office and give them the fax does anything we do even matter?).

Headed over to a friend. Another old building. Those elevators took forever to show up. After a long wait I caught an empty one, and just as the doors were closing a young hand shot out and held the door open.

Two women slowly entered—a young home attendant puzzled by a voice mail on her cell phone, and the other a tiny little old lady as fragile as a dandelion, and obviously loved enough to be dressed well and smell clean.

The little dandelion leaned on her walker and looked at me—that sweet little girl look that often comes back with dementia. I smiled at her. I smiled because I knew few people did. Old age is what cancer used to be—if you don't look it in the eye, it will never happen to you.

Such loneliness. To be visible and not be seen.

The two women got off at their floor, the home attendant gently guiding the little dandelion out. But once in the hallway, the dandelion stopped and, befuddled, pushed her walker back toward the elevator.

As the door closed, I heard the young home attendant gently coaxing her: "Florence. Florence. This way. It's this way home."

LOVE LETTERS TO THE
BORDER OF DESTITUTE

This is Florence somewhere in Bushwick. She told me she could tell how their fortunes were diminishing by how bad the new home was. This move was one of the bigger steps down.

It was illegal for truck drivers to take both the furniture and their owners to wherever they were moving. But Gramma had no way and no money to get from Trenton to Brooklyn and the border of destitute. So the truck driver took pity on the two of them, and they all rode together in the front of his truck to the new apartment.

I know nothing of that apartment on Patchen Avenue, except that Florence flourished at Erasmus High School, was neighbors with someone who knitted mittens used for shooting rabbits, and had someone mail her a little letter so that she could have this special stamp for her collection.

C.O. Moed

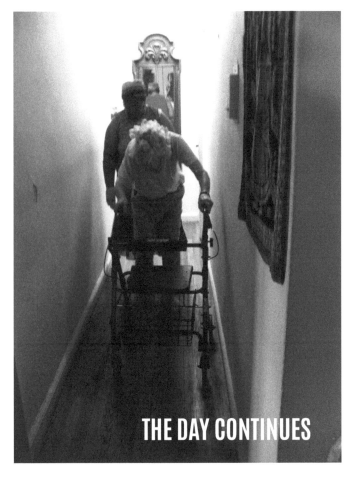

THE DAY CONTINUES

Lunch is done.

I pull out the new Medicaid walker. None of us are strong enough to pick Florence up anymore. Especially when she does that "I-gotta-sit-down-on-the-floor/sidewalk/doctor's office/stairwell/lobby" thing.

That walker is our safety net. It has a chair and it can hold her weight on its arms better than me or my sister or Penny or Gabriella. Beats calling 911 or the Maintenance Guys to pick her up.

Florence does not see it that way. She hates that walker like I hated the violin. And she is seriously pissed off about having to use it. So I sell it like the masterful liar I've become, and tell her that if she uses the walker she'll get strong again and can then tell us all to go to hell. And after she tells us all to go to hell, she can live by herself again and go to dances with lots of girls ready to foxtrot with her and then run up and down Sixth Avenue eating whatever fast food specials she wants.

She grabs those handles and starts shoving herself through space. Penny hovers in the back, prepared to catch her if forward becomes backward, and I shout things at her like "You're doing great" and "Let's go! You're strong! Go Florence!"

Florence is as bad a driver as me, and neither of us can get the walker through one doorway and into another without banging into walls, the desk, bookcases, and every chair in the apartment.

At some point we all give up. Penny settles Florence into the big chair in front of the TV and heads off to her first break in forty-eight hours. I put on *The Parent Trap* with Lindsay Lohan because I don't have anything left inside to watch *Singing in the Rain* for the thirtieth time. I just don't.

The Parent Trap is a miserable movie for both of us. She can't follow it because there is no music to take her through a familiar story. I wince at the bad writing and crude acting, but marvel at the young Lohan and answer Florence's repeated questions about the title the plot the actors the title the plot the actors the title the plot and soon it's over . . .

. . . and I surrender and put on *Singing in the Rain* and Florence sings furiously along, each and every note and soon to hell with Gene Kelly wherever he is in the song. She motions me to join in and I sing along with her " . . . in the rain, what a glorious feeling . . ."

"YOU'RE NOT SINGING IT IN TUNE!" she yells.

APRIL SHOWERS

Only a couple of friends could convince me to leave the East Village. Somehow one did, and on a sunny afternoon I ended up in the middle of nature at a ramshackle house with a long picnic table booming with food, almost too much to drink, and smart minds to enjoy. Didn't know a lot of people. All the old friends were hanging out with one another in the kitchen. Which is how I found myself unexpectedly alone with another guest.

She was a New York sparrow. Looked delicate and cute, but was tough as nails, could survive anything and had.

It wasn't the champagne that got us talking. We recognized each other like war veterans recognize each other. Oh yeah, you were there too? That awful, sometimes slow, but often much-too-fast changing of places when you become your mother and your mother becomes your daughter? Yeah. Me too.

So, filling our glasses some more, she told me her story:

Years ago, the Sparrow's mother fell ill and the Sparrow found herself taking care of her. Not a problem—she was retired and there was some money to get extra help.

But as things progressed, taking a shower at the mother's home soon became not an option. The tub was insurmountable, the shower stall too small for the walker.

One day the mother and the Sparrow got invited to a home that had a shower stall big enough to accommodate the walker.

The sponge baths had been OK, but to have a real shower . . . could the Sparrow give her a shower? The mother asked.

Can you imagine having to ask your child to bathe you?

The Sparrow said of course. Of course she would.

And as soon as she said that she realized this shower would require her to be in the stall with her mother. That was an intimacy they had never before shared.

It wasn't that they didn't like each other or love each other. They did very much so. But it wasn't that kind of warm and physical affection so often seen on *Leave It to Beaver* or *The Partridge Family*. Or even *Star Trek*.

So the Sparrow packed a swimsuit so she could get in the shower with her mom.

When the time came and the mother was carefully wheeled into the stall on her waterproof walker and the water was pouring down, the Sparrow, snug in her suit, stepped into the shower.

There is a moment with an ailing, elderly parent where their sudden nakedness fills your eyes. But that nakedness goes way beyond skin and breasts and scrotum and tufts of hair in quiet places. That nakedness marks the moment you never get to be their child again.

At that moment, the Sparrow told me, the privilege of being a daughter ended right then and there. That privileged role now lived in rounded shoulders, paper-thin fragile skin, a hand full of tremors and very tired eyes. The only thing that mattered was the need to be clean and not be humiliated in the process . . .

. . . and the Sparrow looked down at her swimsuit and wondered what it was about seeing her mother naked and having her mother see her naked. She was sixty, her mother near ninety. What was it that had put the suit between them in the first place?

She slipped the suit off and, with both of them now naked, she began to gently soap up her mom. And as she did, they both started to laugh and weep and laugh and weep and laugh and the water poured out of the shower and the tears poured out of their hearts and there was no difference between them.

THE DANGLING CONVERSATION

Florence doesn't want to go out. What does she want to do? I ask.

"Listen to myself."

What do you hear when you listen to yourself?

"Not much . . . weak and commonplace."

I will come visit you again, I tell her.

"First come by yourself so there's nothing in my way when I tell you how awful you are. . . . That's a joke."

I know.

"I have to work on it."

Heading to Thanksgiving dinner alone, I hear Simon and Garfunkel singing about how each day Florence fades into shadow and I only catch glimpses of her in our dangling conversation.

C.O. Moed

BLOOD ON THE TRACKS

It was so cold and so late and so far uptown, too far uptown when it was that cold and that late.

All of us waiting on the platform did that precarious tipping over like a little teapot as we stared down the dark tunnel hoping the IRT would zoom into sight because our eyeballs were magnets and it just couldn't resist the pull.

That's when I saw the MTA guy walking the tracks, swinging his lantern and flashing his flashlight.

He moved slow, scrutinizing every inch of all the metal and concrete and third rail and pools of floating garbage. Nothing broke his steady stride, not even the rat running across his path in an attempt to avoid him. Behind him were three other men, also swinging lanterns and flashing flashlights and walking steady and slow.

I got that sinking feeling of oh shit the way they're walking no train will be coming like forever.

Then in slow motion the first guy turned and waved his lantern.

Out of nowhere, a train appeared.

All the guys strolled toward the pillars. The train tooted its horn.

"Hey, what are you looking for?" I called out to the first guy.

He wasn't even near his pillar. Just stopped and gave me a long look. Then said, "Everything."

Lying at his feet was the body of a dead rat in a pool of blood.

"Like that?" I asked.

Another long look. The train was practically in the station. "Yeah. A lot of those."

And with that he disappeared into pillars and the blur of a train headed downtown.

C.O. Moed

III SCHERZO

A RIVER IN EGYPT

It doesn't matter that, after deciding somewhere deep inside to never stand on her own two feet again, Florence hasn't walked in months. We kept all her shoes.

Maybe, just maybe, one day, after all the massages and physical therapy and coaxing, just maybe through the open window a breeze will come dancing around her and remind her of the outside wonderfulness she used to stride through.

And maybe, just maybe, she'll put her shoes on again and return to her own two feet.

Florence used to say denial wasn't to be sniffed at.

C.O. Moed

ON THE ROAD

Once upon a time Florence married my father, Seymour, who, according to the love letters I found of his, loved Florence madly.

Growing up, and even after leaving for our own homes, my sister and I so rarely mentioned him that people assumed he had died. He might as well have. Living with a broken heart can feel like a living death.

The Ex-Lover told me that Florence married him because one day the Ex-Lover told her it was time they join the "real" world, marry men, and get on with the life they were supposed to live.

After they divorced thirty years later, Florence described Seymour as her "first hus-*band*." I never got the joke.

Still, before it all went to pot, my parents' early days were carefree and fun, as seen in this picture where they are biking, jaunty jolly, along the old East River Drive by the Williamsburg Bridge, a cigarette dangling out of Seymour's mouth and another dangling from Florence's hand.

My parents always biked. Not on any special mountain bike or with fifteen speeds to pick from, not in any special lane, not with high-tech helmets or fancy spandex or little toe-clip shoes.

My parents rode sturdy Raleigh bikes with an L.L.Bean saddlebag on the back. Gear didn't get fancier than regular shoes or sneakers.

They went places.

Just married, Seymour turned to Florence and said, "Let's go!" Without supplies or extra clothes, they traveled for days. Later, Florence wrote excitedly to the Ex-Lover telling her that after several days, their clothes had become unbearably dirty. Arriving in Philadelphia, Seymour went into Wanamaker's—which was no cheap place—and bought her an entire outfit of new clothes. Both of them barely out of poverty, this was a big deal. (Even after my father had a full-time job, my sister and I could count on one hand the times we bought new clothes.)

My parents traveled up and down the East Coast, the Jersey shore, and all over New York City. And when I was twelve, I too took to the road on one of their Raleighs, biking to babysitting, the youth center on Twelfth Street, and Washington Square Park. Settled in my own apartment in the East Village at seventeen, I commuted to City College up in Harlem with my violin strapped to my back, occasionally with a cigarette dangling from my mouth. No helmet, no fancy spandex. Regular shoes or sneakers.

Florence quit smoking in her fifties, but she continued to bike into her late sixties until I think the bike got stolen and she couldn't replace it. That or we sold it or gave it away because she wasn't wearing a helmet.

Pissed at having to give up the bike, Florence discovered the upside of walking through the city—getting to eat fast food "up and down Sixth Avenue!"

C.O. Moed

ON THE WAY TO GET THE CAT SHAVED

In the middle of all the madness, the small cat living with me grew from something manageable into an eighteen-pound eunuch with matted hair. The Internet said that was bad.

That meant shoving said eunuch into a huge plastic box that has a handle on it to give the illusion a human being could actually pick the box up while there was an animal inside.

No, you cannot.

I get that one's arms are too short to box with God. Mine were also definitely too short to carry this plastic box. Staggering to the corner to get a taxi looked like a scene out of Benny Hill, only not as funny and much more dangerous to anyone within a two-foot radius. Also, it didn't help that once again I heard Florence's voice screaming at me, "YOU'RE TAKING ANOTHER TAXI? STOP TAKING TAXIS!"

If my legs were broken, I had bullet holes up and down my body, and I had to get the winning lottery ticket to the lottery authorities in order to collect a billion dollars, AND I only had ten minutes to do all that, Florence would still yell at me for taking a taxi. However, all I had was a big cat in a heavy plastic box and not enough of my life left to make it onto the Avenue D crosstown bus.

Jumping out of the way of marauding cars flying by at ninety miles an hour and watching a sea of yellow cabs already filled with paying customers whoosh by, my heart and my arms sank.

Until this bright shiny new van-like taxi flashed lights at me from all the way on the other side of the avenue and then somehow, without crashing into anything, cut across four lanes of traffic to pull up to the corner.

Usually with a big cat in a big plastic box, the taxi drivers just wanted to know if their back seat was going to be the same after I left.

But every once in a while, slipping into a taxi's back seat was like running into a neighbor of forty years at the supermarket or bumping into an old pal at the bar.

And it was no different stepping into the chariot of Mr. E from Ghana, who immediately wanted to know everything about the very unhappy beast banging about. Mr. E also wanted to know if I could direct him to where I was going as he had only been on the job for a month.

Mr. E loved being in New York! Mr. E loved driving a taxi in New York! Mr. E loved the United States government because at least when there was corruption here you could do something about it! In Ghana? Mr. E just rolled his eyes and then told short horror stories of bribes and injustice.

But back to more wonderful and happy things to talk about! Mr. E loved animals! Because back in Ghana he had been a farmer with a degree from the university in animal husbandry. And yes, one day he would like to practice that here, maybe even in New York.

Was there anything he missed? I asked.

Leaving his animals, he told me. Including his twenty-two ducks.

We arrived at the cat-shaving place. It was time to say goodbye, but not before telling Mr. E he must, he *just must* get his animal husbandry license here.

We need more citizens who hate corruption and love their animals, especially their twenty-two ducks.

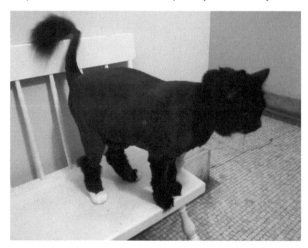

C.O. Moed

STILL HOME

Another day of sitting together watching a movie we had already seen a couple of hundred times. This week it was not *Singing in the Rain*. It was *Sister Act*.

Usually we just sat there watching, Florence holding my hand and me thinking about what to eat after I left.

Suddenly she turned to me and asked, "When do we go home?"

This I wasn't expecting.

"We are home," I answered.

I was hoping that would comfort her, but instead, she got an utterly bewildered look on her face, like a little kid suddenly in a car accident and not understanding what was happening.

Whoopi started singing or doing something nun-like, and Florence went back to watching. But I couldn't go back to dreaming of carbohydrates and their fried friends.

I wasn't ready for this new "normal." I was ready for her to get better. Get better, take back her home, yell at me, stomp around the city.

So I asked, "Do you know who I am?"

Her face got that terrible look again.

Desperate, I blurted out, "Do you know who Louise is?"

Louise. Her other daughter. My older sister. The one who got Florence her first checking account after the divorce, set up the bills, organized the teaching schedule, got the accounts in order, protected Florence's meager assets from disappearing, made sure Florence's name was on things it should be and our names were on the other things, got paperwork in before the laws changed, put together chamber music get-togethers, gave her her first birthday party and birthday cake at sixty-five, had her at the table of every holiday and get-together, made sure Florence would never be homeless . . . Louise. Who ran things so well, Florence was safe, protected, OK.

Florence paused. Then she turned to me and tentatively answered, "Our boss?"

Somewhere, deep, deep, deep inside, my mom was still home.

**THE HOTEL'S
LADIES ROOM**

All day the Hotel Ladies Room Attendant listened to other people go to the bathroom. I know because about twice a week in between therapy sessions and work, I hung out by the makeup mirrors.

She wore a quasi-maid's uniform, repeatedly offering paper towels in broken English that belied sharpness and insight that only comes when you have to start life over in a different country and a different language at the age of forty or fifty or sixty.

Rather than deal with intelligence that could hear them in their most intimate moments, the thousands of perkily dressed mid-management women from out of town strutting power suits for their New York conference summarily dismissed her—day in, day out.

One even demanded to know what that smell was and, at the risk of being complained about, the Hotel Ladies Room Attendant shrugged a very polite fuck-you-lady shrug and said "It's a bathroom."

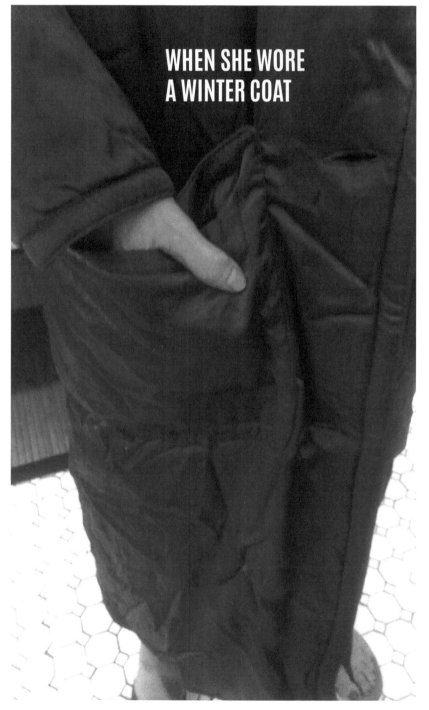

WHEN SHE WORE A WINTER COAT

On the Avenue A bus, Florence was known as the Lady in the Sweater. That's because once the marriage was over, she never wore a winter coat again. We are not quite sure what the connection was between our father and winter coats, but that was that. No matter how bitter it got, how low the thermometer dropped, how hard the snow snowed, Florence wore a sweater and an old scarf.

Years of yelling at her over the phone that it was cold outside, she was sick, and it was fucking us all up when she didn't take care of herself had no effect whatsoever.

Until . . .

In her late sixties, early seventies, she started giving piano lessons in people's homes. Charging barely more than twenty dollars, she trudged from apartment to apartment—old walk-ups and fancy new high-rises—lugging a bag packed with Xeroxed piano tunes that aimed not to teach piano but to entertain excited adults who always wanted to play a popular tune and a lot of young children usually less enthusiastic about music lessons than their parents, thrilled to have a seemingly harmless old lady—graduate of Juilliard—piano teacher who came cheap.

The students for the most part were native New Yorkers or bohemians or used to different drummers and different beats. So Florence showing up without a winter coat was just a minor detail when talking about the elderly piano teacher who made house calls.

Except for one family. They were rich; they were powerful; they were used to seeing their name on different buildings throughout the city. And an old lady showing up with a bag full of Xeroxes and not

C.O. Moed

wearing anything but a sweater and scarf was not acceptable.

Which is why Florence began to receive winter coats from them every holiday season. Really, really nice ones. With really, really high-end labels.

Hating each and every one of these garments, she would, as the weather began to turn cold, grimly drag one on in a fury and stomp off to teach this family's kids. As soon as the lesson was over, she'd stomp home and the coat would stay in the closet until it was time for her to stomp on back the following week.

At some point, the family stopped asking her to teach their kids. Although she missed the money, not wearing the coat was a "fucking relief." Knowing that I was always cold, did wear winter coats, and was usually too broke to buy a nice one, she passed two on to me.

No matter how warm the coats were, Florence's history of going from home to home, laden with cheap songs and attempting to make a living while holding onto what was left of her soul, left me chilled. But I was cold. So I wore one into the ground. The other one—long, warm, fancy—came down to my ankles, and one day I decided I'd rather be cold than looking so ridiculous.

Out of the blue, a tall friend with an easy demeanor mentioned she needed a winter coat, something nice and long. As easy as it was for Florence to slip that coat off and be freed from it, I slipped it on my friend and suddenly there was no history or sorrow. Just a beautiful warm coat perfect for when the weather turned.

A WOMAN'S BED WHERE SHE LIES WITH POEMS

t's rumored to be made of horsehair, this bed she has slept in since 1977.

Bought it with the only girlfriend she ever lived with (and eventually dumped for the Ex-Lover and their wild reunion fling when they were both in their sixties).

I think there was even a story of this girlfriend and Florence giggling like mad when they brought this queen-size mattress into the building because all the neighbors were watching and knew something different was happening behind closed doors. (Or maybe that was the Christmas tree story, another act of terrorism that only two middle-aged lesbians could do in a Jewish enclave.)

I have never laid down on this bed.

I have stripped it, cleaned it, made it. I have sprayed it with Febreze. I have sat on it, held Florence's hand, and comforted her on this bed. I have dressed her, undressed her, and clipped her nails on this bed. And every time, thinking she was back in the tenement on Hester Street where sleepovers were common between friends, Florence would invite me to "lie down and go to sleep" on this bed.

Her bed.

C.O. Moed

The bed she bought to begin a new life, new hope, new love. The bed where she promised herself better futures and denied worse pasts. The bed no man ever slept in.

The bed where she cradled herself through sleep, the radio playing all night NPR news shows. The bed she loved in, climaxed in, lost love in, splintered peace with frightening dreams in, refused to cry in. Cried in.

Her bed. Filled with poems fiercely recited as reality shattered and disappointment flooded in.

Tomorrow the Medicaid electric hospital bed will arrive. Its hydraulic lift will make bed-bathing Florence less backbreaking for Gabriella and Penny. It will have bars to keep Florence from falling out in the middle of the night. It will have buttons that push Florence up to sitting and down to sleeping. And when it is no longer needed, it will be returned to Medicaid.

Tomorrow Gabriella and I will somehow coax Florence from her old bed. I will lie, not on her bed, but to her face.

I will say: "We are putting you in a special bed just for a little while. Until you get better and can sit up without being dizzy. And when you do get better and when you are walking again, you'll go lay down in your own bed and then we will go to Coney."

And she will correct me and say "Coney ISLAND. And I will LIE down, not LAY down."

And I will nod and know my lie is forever.

**HEAVY
LIFTING:
GABRIELLA**

C.O. Moed

Sleep-in Medicaid Home Attendants work sixty hours straight around the clock. They get paid for thirty. Because technically they aren't really "working" when the person they are taking care of around the clock is sleeping. Not sure who Medicaid thinks is taking care of the sick person at night. Maybe the fairies?

During waking hours, the Home Attendants are shopping, cooking, feeding, dressing, coaxing, cleaning butts, and dodging interactions that are less than pleasant—like being spit at, grabbed at, cursed at, treated like a mistake God made. And yet, these almost-all-women show up for work, day in and day out, to care for people others can't or won't care for.

Louise and I couldn't afford to stop our jobs or, in her case, also child care. Applying for Medicaid was a battle a brilliant private caseworker took on for us. She was a pitbull. And the folks at the Medicaid offices and helplines and Social Security offices were pretty wonderful too, whispering to me what I really needed to do to make sure Florence was treated fairly, taken care of. We found out only later we were one of the very few who got twenty-four-hour home care during those days.

But being awarded care was just the beginning. Our local agency around the corner had to find folks who were willing to take the job. After some disastrous attempts—because who wants to be spit at, flailed at, and called names, Penny and Gabriella came in, and somehow Florence didn't hate them.

Penny was the boss and we all deferred to her. It wasn't just easier. She was definitely smarter than us. She knew the best way to do just about everything.

Gabriella, on the other hand, was like visiting someone wonderful in a beautiful garden—a chance to breathe deep and ponder things.

She had been a schoolteacher in Haiti. Maybe that's why Florence relaxed with her—the rare combination of being with someone sharp and smart like she was, but much nicer, making it feel like home was as kind as second grade when things were briefly safe.

And Gabriella literally did the heavy lifting. Like picking Florence up from the ground when she collapsed. Repeatedly. And helping her have a successful bowel movement. And getting Florence to get out of bed when she refused. And feeding and cooking and shopping and laundry which was on the other side of the housing project and . . .

She was also the bearer of news that we didn't want to get, telling us it was time to come up with other bathing/cleaning strategies because it was too dangerous to get Florence in and out of the tub.

She was the one who told us it was time to get a wheelchair because Florence could no longer walk more than a few steps before hitting the ground.

And she was the one who broke it to me gently it was time for a hospital bed. That way it would be easier to clean Florence with the baby wipes without hurting her or Penny's backs. And it would keep Florence safe.

I couldn't get a lot of stories from her, and she didn't think it was allowed for pictures to be taken of her on the job. All I know is for sixty hours a week, 3,600 minutes, 216,000 seconds in a dusty old beat-up apartment, no breaks, no company except a frustrated and frustrating old woman, with the trains running all day and night on the Williamsburg Bridge, she took care of Florence with a compassion that repeatedly made my heart break.

And what else I know is that when I met her husband picking her up one day, I wanted whoever I married to look at me the way he looked at her.

TOO LATE, TOO EARLY, NEVER ON TIME

I t is yet another doctor's appointment.

Gabriella and I do that mad dash at less than zero miles per hour of getting Florence into the wheelchair and then into the elevator and then I run down the five flights of stairs while Gabriella rides down in the elevator with Florence because there is only room for one wheelchair and one healthy person in it and then we all meet on the ground floor and then I run outside and wave to the Maintenance Guys to let them know we are here and then they go get the ramp and bring it into the lobby for those two stairs we just can't seem to manage without Florence flying out onto the floor and then we all get to the lobby door and wait for the Maintenance Guys to pick up the ramp and put it down the steps in front of the building, and then we get down those steps and then go running as fast as we can without Florence flying out of the wheelchair and we get to the corner of Broome and Columbia.

C.O. Moed

And there's the Delancey Car Service guy. Glaring at us like *Hey. Five minutes ago, I said three minutes* and I whip out that smile, the one I greet everyone with when I have to enlist them to help me take care of Florence, and I smile that big smile like *Isn't she cute this little old lady look how much I'm caring for my old mother aren't we a sympathetic sight?*

This guy doesn't give a shit. He just cares he has to wait in the cold or the hot or the rain or the whatever and he is sick of waiting. So then Gabriella does extra fussing over Florence so that he knows, HE KNOWS, how fragile she is and how we had to do so much just to get to the goddamn corner.

And then, finally, Florence is in the car and the wheelchair is in the trunk and Gabriella is waving goodbye and headed for a much-needed break and we are off and speeding to the hospital's Curb of Insanity and yet another doctor's appointment for yet another something that has gone wrong with a body that is slowly giving up on itself.

We get there not only on time but early, which is what you gotta do—I mean even if you are late for the car service (which no matter what you do you are always late for) you are always on time or early for the doctor appointment because the doctors at this hospital's clinic are always running late.

This day is no exception. The waiting room is packed with every kind of geriatric infirmity. Doesn't matter what God you pray to or the color of the skin you live in or what language you speak or where you come from. Old age is a brutal equal opportunity motherfucker. And the only difference in how you die is money. You got money, you don't go to a hospital's outpatient clinic and sit for hours in a packed waiting room.

You got Medicaid? You do. But at least you get great doctors who give a shit, and, in my book, that makes me and Florence fucking lucky. And we are even more lucky than lucky. We got money for a car service, so we don't have to wait in the cold or the hot or the rain or the whatever to take the Avenue A or D buses.

For a second I breathe a sigh of relief and give thanks for what we got and how we got to where we got to and now all we have to do is sit here and wait for some doctor to probe Florence and talk to her like she is old or human before we reverse the madness and go from point B back to point A.

Florence suddenly looks up and quietly says to me: "I have to go to the bathroom."

"OK," I quietly say back. Get up to wheel her to the nearest bathroom built for walkers and wheelchairs. And just as I'm about to maneuver her out of our corner, she quietly says, "I think it's too late."

I didn't know there was a difference in how you push a wheelchair when it's "I have to go to the bathroom" and "I think it's too late." But suddenly I know the difference and I cut through that crowded waiting room like a samurai sword slicing a bologna sandwich straight into the big clean bathroom

Door locked, dump my coat in the corner, and then gently push down Florence's sweatpants to see what the damage is . . .

. . . and it's Spectacular. Filling everything between skin and cloth to capacity, and with that reveal, a smell immediately fills the bathroom to capacity.

And there is Florence. A look of resignation, complete helplessness but something else. Something new. A look of trust, that I was going to take care of her, and I wasn't going to yell at her like how she used to yell at me when I peed in the bed or in my pants. She just knew. And of course, *of course* I wasn't going to yell at her. But how did I learn to mother like that? There must have been some brief moments, tiny fissions, miniscule cracks where she cared for me as I was suddenly caring for her.

It takes a lot of finesse and skillful juggling to get a pair of cheap cotton sweatpants off and then a pair of beat-up cotton panties holding a family-size salad bowl of feces into a small garbage can with only some of it going on the floor.

Then it takes a lot a lot a lot of something from deep inside, I don't even know what it is, to get an eighty-four-year-old battered little girl to sit quietly on the toilet while I clean up the floor with soap and the few remaining paper towels.

And then there is the attempt at cleaning the sweatpants in the sink with the dollop of soap given each time I activate the infrared portion control. I just want to get them clean enough to be worn again in a doctor's office without me being charged with neglect or senior abuse. And then there's drying of the sweatpants under the hand dryer, so they are dry enough for Florence to sit in them without getting pneumonia.

And then there's the tushy cleaning. There's enough toilet paper for this so it's now only about getting the water not too hot or not too cold (which in these hospital bathrooms means very tepid to miserable) and then doing my best to keep the toilet paper from totally disintegrating. It takes almost all the toilet paper to get most of the feces that went all over her backside and beyond reasonably gone and all I have to do is somehow clean the toilet seat while she is still on it because I can't put her back in the wheelchair until the sweatpants are only slightly damp.

At this point it's been twenty-three minutes because I'm counting how late the doctors are running and if they are going to call our name and then cancel us if we don't answer. The floor and Florence are almost kinda clean but there is no air freshener in the world that can take care of the smell emanating from that tiny garbage can in that tiny room.

At last the sweats are now only slightly damp, and I pull them back up her now kinda clean tushy, get my hands soapy and wash hers with mine, and dry them with my T-shirt. And then one more time wipe down this geographical landscape of humanness with what's left of the toilet paper, which is falling apart with every swipe.

Finally, I open the bathroom door and come face-to-face with a very pissed-off nurse who, I think, was maybe expecting one of the many homeless who sneak into these public bathrooms to clean themselves. The smell tells her we could be, but since we don't have a ton of bags with us, she looks confused.

"I'm so sorry, but there was an accident," I say with my best embarrassed-exhausted-overwhelmed demeanor of a child taking care of her parent, which is not a hard stretch. I actually *am* an embarrassed-exhausted-overwhelmed child taking care of her parent.

The nurse's very pissed-off look turns into full-out exasperation. I wish I could glare at people like that. But then again, that would blacklist me and Florence from every doctor's office on the eastern seaboard. There's no Medicaid in the world that could make that better.

After explaining and pleading and pleading again, the front desk keeps our appointment for us, even though we didn't answer when they called for us ten minutes ago. We wait another forty-five minutes without any more accidents. Which is a relief because there is now nothing between Florence's tushy and the wheelchair except a not-quite-clean, cheap, thin, damp pair of sweatpants.

From that day on, no matter where we go, even to just outside the lobby door, I pack extra underwear, sweatpants, and baby wipes.

And Florence starts wearing diapers.

HOME, HOME, HOME ON THE RANGE

'm so beat, I tell people I am only willing to leave my neighborhood for the promise of romance or the guarantee of food. Two old friends call me. They aren't promising me love but they swear a great meal awaits me in Flushing. Sometimes, that's just as good. I grab my metro card and head out.

But of course, the 7 Train isn't doing Manhattan this weekend so I transfer from the BMT at Queensboro Plaza to get to Main Street. A billion people mill around as this MTA guy stands on the platform, shouting into the megaphone about the 7 Train changes and where to transfer to where and what to do and . . .

Three hours later—and so well fed, the hell with love—I head back to the city. The same MTA guy is still there, still shouting into the megaphone about the 7 Train changes and where to transfer to where and what to do and . . .

"I'm just delivering the information—they can receive it or not." But he admits that after nine hours of this, well, he is just going to have to pray and give it to God when he sings in church the next day.

The train comes and we all surge on, grabbing seats, a gaggle of boys hanging off the handrail, speaking to each other in something that sounds like Korean but I know isn't. One gets sassy with me. He thinks I'm just an old lady and will be too nervous to tell him if I find his friend's haircut attractive. So I tell him that I had the same cut in the 1980s including the fade in the back, and he goes and figures out I was born in the '60s. Close enough.

"I'm good at math, I'm Asian."

I roll my eyes and they tell me they're headed to a party, they're from Tibet, they're arguing about which stop to get off, there will be girls there and they keep asking me if I think haircut boy is cute.

Finally, I shrug. "He seems like a good-looking kid." And the kid goes, "I'm nineteen!" And I go, "I'm old enough to be your grandmother, you're a kid."

All of them laughing and pushing and fixing their many different haircuts trying not to look too fussy, I say to the sassy kid, "You want to know how to get a girl interested in you? Listen to her." And him nodding but hoping he doesn't have to do much more to get her to kiss him.

And the boys rush out to somewhere in Queens, and the family who also got on at Queensboro Plaza all sit down— the mom, the older sister who looks just like the mom, the fierce little brother, and the calm middle sister who had to ask the screaming MTA guy for directions because her mother didn't speak enough English.

I pull out my sock knitting and the middle girl asks me what I'm doing and who I'm making them for and is it hard to do, and the older sister takes out their new pet, a beta fish they got at the ninety-nine-cent store but it cost seven dollars, they named her Vanessa.

And I tell them about my fishes Esmerelda, Harold, and Skuzy, and the fierce little brother comes closer because he wants to hear about how my fish all loved each other, and they all get off at Thirty-Fourth Street waving goodbyes and I miss them already, and I'm home as I go home.

C.O. Moed

THE NOT-ON-TV OFFICE: WHEN DUTY CALLS

'm not the only one at work doing a juggling act.

Tee just got a call from her son. Seems her father, Daddy, just fired the third home aide in two months. Hired another one recommended by one of his friends—either the one who can't walk or the one who can't see. This new home attendant arrived by Access-A-Ride in her scooter. The scooter couldn't get in the house, so Daddy sent her for coffee.

"Oh shit," Daddy told the son. "I fucked up."

He's still flushing food down the toilet, won't take off his woolen hat no matter how hot it gets, says mean, mean stuff, and keeps telling everyone Tee is either not helping him at all or trying to kill him, depending on the day and which company is visiting. He refuses to be evaluated for anything because he's not crazy, everyone else is.

Daddy is a vet. World War II. So that means the Veterans Administration will pay for a nursing home. And sometimes the visiting nurse service for a couple of weeks. That's it. Nothing else. No home aide, no housekeeper, no food stamps. No nothing. Everything outside of the nursing home is out of pocket. His pocket. Tee's pocket.

Tee and her sister write down everything Daddy does that lets them know something is wrong. But just like me and Louise with Florence, how do you prove something is wrong when that's how they've always acted? I tell Tee, "Well, sometimes you gotta wait until they start peeing on themselves and can't wipe anymore."

Tee takes care of his part of the house, her part of the house, the kids, the grandkids, her husband. Tee is tired. Real tired. But just like me and Louise before we fought with Medicaid and won, what does it mean to be a good daughter? Where does You stop and Daughter begin? Where does Daughter stop and You begin?

I tell Tee you kick out the rage on a wall, and every day swear to take nothing personal just keep saying if it was cancer I wouldn't take the tumor personal, so why am I taking personal familiar words coming out of a brain eating itself alive?

THE BIG QUESTION GAME! or DIFFERENT DAY, SAME S#*T

Link up the real person to the real question really asked in the last couple of days:

A. Should we go to the ER?	1. Gabriella
B. Do you think she has pneumonia or is it just a cold?	2. Me
C. What are you going to do if you get sick or injured?	3. Former boss
D. Do you want extra time off for your birthday?	4. Florence
E. Where is our house?	5. Old friend
F. Is your father still alive?	6. Me

Answers: Does it really matter?

C.O. Moed

STAIRWAY TO HEAVEN

We didn't call it *Low-ssss* like it was some royal palace. We called it *Low-eeez*. Because that's how you really say "Loews."

Low-eeez.

This one was on Delancey Street. So we called it *da Low-eeez Delancee* (as opposed to the one on Grand Street and Essex, which was smaller). And it was no royal palace. It was a beat-up movie theater with a tattered lobby.

"Where ya goin'?"

"Low-eez Delancee. Gonna go see a pitcha."

Florence told me when she was a girl—and even as a young woman—she used to climb up the fire escape stairs and sneak into the movie house to see the second feature because it was easier to sneak in during the second half. It was easier to sneak in, period. No fire alarm, no cameras, no nothing.

I remember me and my sister going to the Saturday matinees, the place packed with screaming kids. The "COMING ATTRACTIONS!" were always horror movie trailers with monsters and demons and really scary men. Maybe there was already too much fear inside me from this life or a past life or the street life but I would freak out and run to the back of the theater and hide in the lobby until "COMING ATTRACTIONS!" were over. For years the words "coming attractions!" sent me into a panic.

On the rare occasion Florence took me along in one of her infrequent escapes, it was understood I was not to bother her or remind her of her current life as mother/wife/piano teacher. I was to be a silent witness. So when I panicked at "COMING ATTRACTIONS!" I tried to be really quiet about it. This was her time, and I now wonder what movie I really watched—the one on the screen or the one sitting next to me.

Who knows what lives inside *da Low-eez Delancee* these days . . . the neighborhood spouting up luxury housing, the street level filled with cheap stores and cheaper national chains. Any hint of a movie theater has been obliterated.

But ghosts of those stairs are still there, etched in brick and holding memories of a rakish girl sneaking in to see a pitcha.

THE LONG AND WINDING ROAD

We all had great hope it would go away. But it didn't.

I was still putting back together the pieces of a recently broken life—I just wanted a bit more time before another ten hours in the ER.

I kept asking Gabriella (with great hope), "Maybe it's a cold?"

Gabriella kept saying, "I don't know."

I couldn't ask Penny, who had opinions on these kinds of things. She was on vacation.

Then Penny's substitute home attendant and the recreational therapist both said something.

I finally asked Doctor Russia (with great hope), "Maybe it's a cold?"

He said, "No, it's not cold. Bring her to ER. It is best. They'll do X-rays . . ."

C.O. Moed

Then Gabriella said (with great hope), "She seems better!"

But the next morning it was still there. And when I got down to her apartment I knew it was not a cold. Her chest heaved up and down like Sigourney Weaver in *Ghostbusters* when she got possessed.

So we began the long and winding . . .

"You're doing great," I told her.

"You're just saying that. I'm a mess," she said.

I couldn't stop laughing. "You're right. You're a mess."

"It's all your fault," she reminded me.

When the ER nurse asked her, "Do you know where you are?"

Florence answered, "I'm not home."

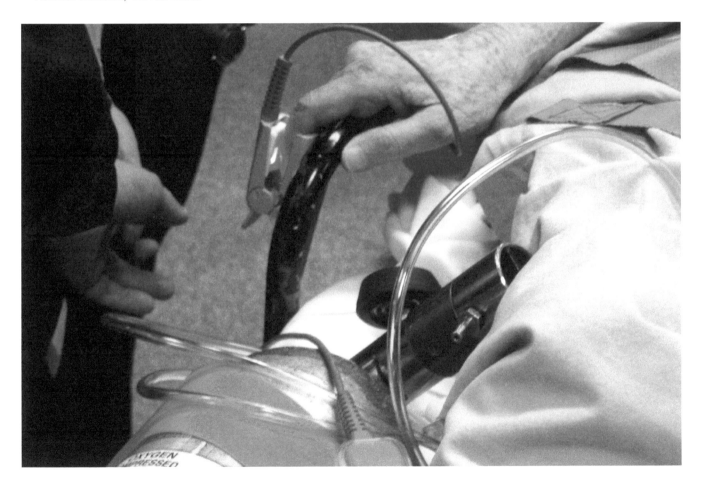

WHEN US TWO WENT A' TRAVELING

W hat to Bring to the ER
    Crackers
    Ensure
    Cups
    Straws
    Water bottle
    Yogurt
    Your own spoon
    Writing work waiting for better words
    Pens and highlighter case
    Filofax with all the numbers to contact in case of _____
    Prayer bag with sutra book and beads
    Extra camera
    Knitting
    L.L.Bean catalog to distract Florence
    Swimming to Antarctica by Lynne Cox to distract me
    Journal to write everything down

C.O. Moed

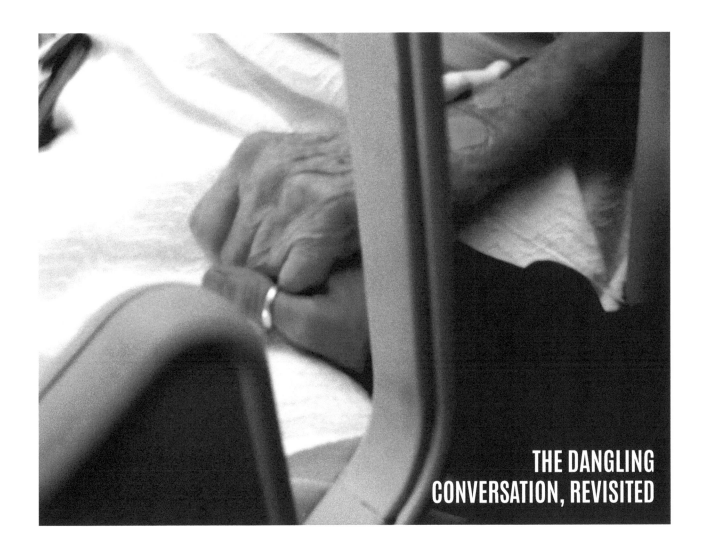

THE DANGLING CONVERSATION, REVISITED

"I have unsettled things in my body."

"Claire. Are you Claire or Louise?"

"I swear if I ever get past here, I'll shoot you."

"When do I get up in the morning?"
Me: When you wake up in the morning.
"Oh fuck."

"I'm not going to say no in this place."

"Did you think a little nothing in the morning could keep me here all day?"

Doctor: Florence, can you tell me where we are? What kind of building is this?
"Oh, it's a swell building."

"I love you."
Me: I love you.
"I never said that to anybody."
Me: I know
"How do you know?"
Me: I know you.

"Help me."
Me: What do you need?
"Somebody's hand."

"Everything will be alright."

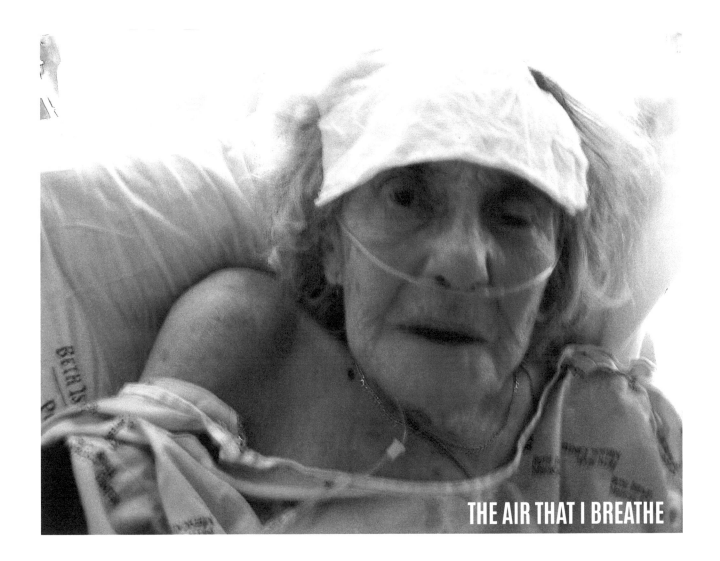

THE AIR THAT I BREATHE

It's 10:30 at night.

Something is wrong.

Even after they give her medicine from a mask that comes pouring out into her face, Florence can't stop coughing *it hurts it hurts* and afterward she is too wiped out to even breathe she begs me *make it better make it better* I keep wetting paper towels beg her to keep the mask with all the medicine pouring out into her face she keeps taking the mask off *it hurts it hurts* she can't breathe it's wiping her out *make it better make it better* I keep wetting paper towels beg her to keep the mask with all the medicine pouring out into her face she keeps taking off the mask off *it hurts it hurts make it better . . .*

Finally, at 11:30 at night . . .

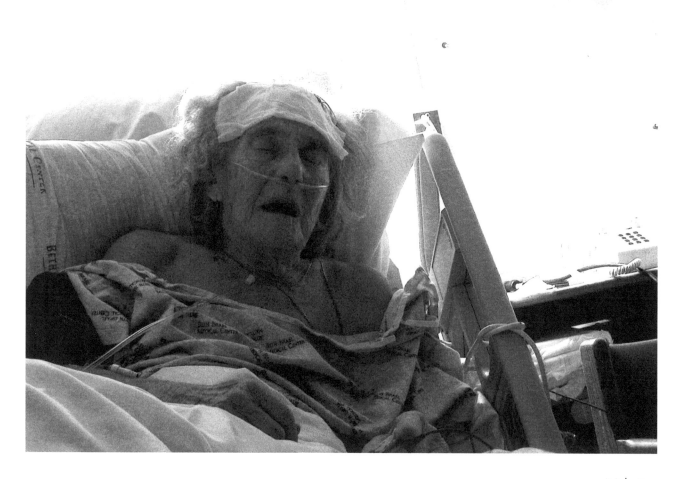

. . . it is better.

C.O. Moed

LITTLE MARIA AND THE TENDER MERCY OF BREAD

Maria is all of teeny tiny. She is across from Florence in Bed 3.

She lives near Florence—Delancey and Essex, or maybe that's where she shops, the Essex Street Market. It's hard to tell. My rudimentary Spanish picks up about half of what she says. The assistant nurse waves it off. "Oh she blabs a lot so don't worry if you don't catch it all."

But this night I come in and she starts talking too fast even after I beg in Spanish "Despacio, por favor, despacio." Because this doesn't feel like blabbing. This feels important and I need to understand.

The other roommate in Bed 1—ninety-five years old, sharp as a tack, used to live on Suffolk and Houston but now is in Brooklyn near Coney because her son has a house—she translates what I miss, not because she understands Spanish, but because she saw what happened.

Florence hadn't been eating for days. Nothing tasted good, everything made her cough, she didn't feel like it. The nurses or the assistant nurses tried to coax a few things down and the other day I got her to gum a piece of chicken and a piece of carrot before she spit it all out. I tried the Ensure but it made her cough. I just couldn't insist. So mostly the food trays stayed untouched.

This particular night had been extra busy. I am not sure why. Maybe more beds got filled or dinners were arriving all at once and the healthy people in charge of the unhealthy people suddenly had their hands full. Whatever the reason, there just weren't enough hands to go around or enough time to make sure everyone got fed. So no one was around to coax Florence to take a second bite or another sip.

Maria got up out of bed, went over to Florence, and fed her.

**Goodnight
My Someone**

In her later years, whenever Florence said goodbye to anyone, she'd give a jaunty wave and sing out, "See you in my dreams!"

So, after getting a message that Florence is being sent home once she is assessed for palliative care, I take this picture. Just in case I don't.

C.O. Moed

OF OLD DIVE BARS

I t was wonderful to be back.

In my absence, they got new barstools you could actually sit on without sliding off the cracked vinyl. But the beautiful lady wasn't living over the cash register anymore.

At least the old wood tables with millions of initials and last words cut into them hadn't been replaced with new shit pretending to be old.

Best of all, still there was that ancient scent of cat pee and dead rats mingling with the same crowd of tough drinkers and tenderhearted writers that I knew since I was a teenager drinking with Florence. Even the young bartender looked familiar. Like out of a photograph from years ago.

"I've been coming here since 1975, 1976," I said.

"Me too," he said.

I laughed. "What, since you were five?"

"Yeah," he said. "My dad is J—."

One of the owners.

Those long-ago afternoons when no one was there, just us regulars drifting in on late-day sun, the *Daily News*, *New York Post* spread out on the bar, Frazier the bartender and a former roommate, flipping through the gossip pages and the sordid stories of crimes that shouldn't have happened, maybe a late lunch, extra sandwich, and a drink on the house for Tommy who lived down the street at one of the Bowery missions. Just the company we needed to keep during those long-ago days.

And every once in a while, two little boys played in the corner as their father checked out the beer pipes and the hundred-year-old wiring.

IN THE STILL OF THE NIGHT

The call from Penny at 2:13 a.m. Something is more wrong than the usual wrong.

    I scramble for clothes . . . no, not that T-shirt! I like that one. I'm always going to remember what I wore this night.

    I throw on a shirt I hate.

The cab driver doesn't realize Columbia stops going two ways at Delancey. He tries to speed on the East River Drive service road but hits all the red lights on Grand.

Does running fast through an empty courtyard in the middle of the night—down the same stone walkway I played on as a child, past the fountain I sat by—does running fast slow down bad things?

Two years of opening Florence's door to a constantly changing "normal"—from a woman who once not only played the complete repertoire of Bach, Beethoven, and Chopin, but also walked to the supermarket on her own—to this moment as a fragile piece of lace held together by ancient skin, struggling to breathe, her only seeing eye already traveling to other places.

When I ask her "Can I take you to the doctor?" the sound "No" shoots out, not from parched lips unable to close for fear of suffocation, but from a gut clinging to home.

So I sing the sutras. She sips some water.

There is still too much distress, I tell Penny. Penny is silent. She knows she can't say anything. It's not her job. It never was.

I pull out the wishes made ten years ago. What decision can I live with, what decision can I not, old papers, words scratched out, others neatly typed . . .

I read them again. What decision can I live with, what decision can I not?

Penny listens, tilts her head, raises her eyebrows, nods, listens, tilts her head, raises her eyebrows, nods . . .

It is near three a.m. Doctor Russia calls back immediately. He assures me if it is another flare-up then the hospital can treat it. He assures me if it is the end I can get her home. He assures me I can refuse intubations. He assures me . . .

It's win-win, I say to Penny. I'm calling 911.

I turn back and murmur to Florence "You are in so much distress I want to take you to the doctor I promise you I'll bring you home I promise you I'll bring you back home I promise you I promise . . ."

"OK" whispered back—her trust in me, her trust—she raised me not to lie.

EMTs appear suddenly. *He* is tall huge like a redwood. *She* is officious. They both stomp around with many big FDNY emergency bags. Two more show up. Such heavy boots. The neighbors below must know something is happening. *She* orders everyone around.

Suddenly Florence, my mother, my charge, my responsibility is suddenly no longer mine. She is *theirs* and I cannot stop them or the massive amount of medical equipment flying out of boxes and bags or the law that says the form we didn't fill out means *they* get to do everything.

When I hear my mother cry out, I snap "No more!" or "Stop that!" or something that attempts to get back my mother, get her back to me. One of them steps in front of me and keeps me from stopping them.

The stretcher doesn't fit in the elevator so they tip her up. If they went a bit higher she'd be on her own two feet for the first time in months.

She tries to put me in the second ambulance.

"No! I'm riding with my mother."

He points to the front seat—I can only ride shotgun, not in the back holding my mother's hand.

She says, "Stop taking pictures please."

"I'm not taking any of you, just my mother."

She says, "It's breaking HIPAA patient confidentiality."

"She's my mother. I am her HIPAA person."

She says, "Ma'am, it's breaking confidentiality."

I mutter under my breath, "I'll take a picture of my mother if I want to." But I'm too tired, too tired, too tired. "I'll take a picture of the coffee cups instead."

He grins. My camera malfunctions.

I hear a siren in the distance and then realize it is ours.

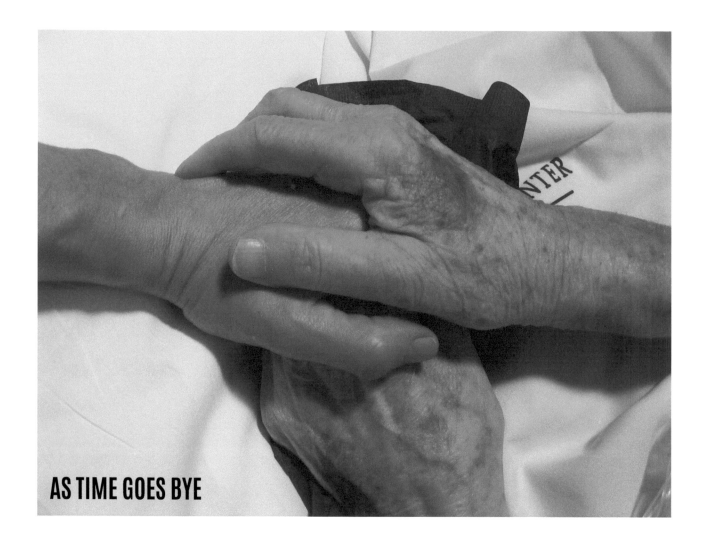

AS TIME GOES BYE

The night Florence and I spent ten hours in the ER, some addict was screaming at a doctor who politely refused him drugs and calmly showed him the door. Tonight he is Florence's ER doctor. And tonight he calmly guided us to a door only Florence could step through.

"Do you understand what that means if we do that? If we remove the intubation tube?"

Yes.

"OK honey, OK, sweetheart, I'm sorry, we're almost done, it's a bit uncomfortable, we're almost done. . . . Your mother was biting the tubes."

Biting?

"Yes. She didn't want them."

I'm glad she was biting them.

"Let's make her as comfortable as possible now."

But I want her home.

"The lab result just came back. It looks like she had a heart attack."

Should I call my sister or can we wait . . . ?

"No, call your sister, now! Tell her to get here as soon as she can!"

"I'm on my way, I'm on my way, I couldn't find any cash for a car service, I'm on the train platform . . ."

Mom, she's on the train platform. You have to hang in there until she gets here. You have to. I know you can do it. Hang in there.

"You're looking at the machine to tell you how your mother is doing. I'm going to turn off the machines so that you can just be with her."

I can't remember the Cole Porter song, "You're the Top." I can't remember it. It's her favorite. I can't remember. I didn't bring her cassette player to play her old songs.

"Do you know when your sister might get here?"

MY MOTHER WILL WAIT! MY MOTHER WILL WAIT! SHE'S GOING TO WAIT UNTIL MY SISTER GETS HERE. MOM, SHE'S ON THE TRAIN PLATFORM, SHE'S ON HER WAY!

"Here. I just downloaded Pandora on my iPhone. It's not all Cole Porter but similar. Here, put it by her ear."

Mom! Louise is here

"Hi Mom."

We're both here, we're both here, we're here, we're here we're here thank you thank you I love you thank you so much for giving me music I'm so grateful I love you music is the most important thing in my life I got so much from thank you for my passion thank you for my art I'm so sorry so grateful so love you so thank you so much so love you so sorry so grateful so love you thank you . . .

I'll SEE YOU IN MY DREAMS

t should have been just another one of our many visits to our local hospital.

Only this time there was no fighting, no singing, no charming the doctors. No admonishing me about how it was all my fault.

No nothing.

There were just the three of us: my sister and me taking turns holding Florence's hand.

Near 6:25 a.m., on the first day of Rosh Hashanah—the beginning of our new year and the anniversary of her first date with the Ex-Lover when they were just teenage girls—with Astaire, Ella, and Sinatra playing into her ear from the very new iPhone of Dr. ER, in some brief second of some brief exhale, Florence, aka Deutschie, died.

My mother never got to go home. She died where she did not want to die.

But she did not die in pain and she did not die in fear. She did not die in a bedroom steeped in decades of misery and disappointment. And she did not die alone or lonely.

Because I lied and never brought her home, she died holding my hand while my sister and I chatted like machine guns about something else in our mother's life we didn't understand, which was just about everything.

Afterward, I stepped into the morning air with knowledge that only comes from absolute endings. I was no longer the child who had failed her, but a woman who survived a decision.

C.O. Moed

IV PRESTO

HYMIE

He was already living across the hall from us the day we moved in in 1961. He never spoke to us kids and us kids never spoke to him, but we knew to be respectful and silent as he came and went.

When Florence got sick fifty years later, I bumped into him more. We started giving each other a slight nod at some point, but mostly it was still that Lower East Side gaze from the corner of our eye, letting the person know *I-see-you-I-still-don't-talk-to-you*.

I was spending yet another sunny day unburying her life from all the papers she kept. Hit a wall, took a break, got a café con leche from the Dominican place that used to be the Giorgianni Brothers market. I needed to cry, and caffeine made it go faster.

There he was, pushing his big shopping cart full of laundry to the lobby door. He pointed to a newly posted death notice, taped to the building.

And then, for the first time, after not a word—not one single word in fifty years—we talked.

"Hannah's brother?" he asked.

C.O. Moed

No, it was Shia on the third floor who died.

"How old?"

Late seventies, because he was younger than Florence.

"Seventies? That's young. I'm ninety-one."

And then after fifty years, and after our very first words, I finally met Hymie.

He takes good care of himself. Sure, his nephew out on Long Island keeps an eye on him. And yeah sure, the Vet Administration tried to give him home aides, but what for? He has Lifeline. "Just like having a person there." Still, the VA's been very good to him. Full disability.

World War II? I asked.

"Yeah. I got captured in France. Was a POW in Germany. Stalag 11B." After the war, all the guys would get together. He doesn't go to the reunions anymore. "Most of them have checked out," he said.

I reached down to help him get his cart up the five scattered steps to the lobby door—the same steps we needed two of the Maintenance Guys to get Florence in and out of the building.

"Nah. I got a system. I'm still pretty strong!" and before I knew it, he bump-bump-bumped the big shopping cart up each step.

The blond mommy and her little blond boy dressed as Robin Hood were coming out of the building. When I was growing up I could count on three fingers all the blond people in the entire neighborhood. Now it's normal.

Seeing the kid, Hymie lit up like a Ferris wheel at night. "Whatcha got there, huh!?"

And then in the time-honored Lower East Side act of loving kids, he pulled out a one-dollar bill (a nickel in my day) and stuffed it in the little boy's hand. "Here! For Halloween!"

The mommy turned to her son. "What do you say?"

"Thank you!" Robin Hood answered promptly, and he and Hymie grinned at each other before the kid and the mommy headed off to Sherwood Forest or maybe the Avenue A bus.

Hymie turned back to me. "I'm going on a cruise."

The nephew out on Long Island taking you someplace warm? I asked.

"Nah." A mischievous twinkle in his eye. "Guess where?! Europe! I'm flying into Rome and then taking a cruise all over Europe. Athens."

With your nephew?

"No. By myself."

I looked so shocked he got this big grin and I saw the young soldier who had grit and guts and verve and survived a POW camp.

"People see an old man alone, they're very helpful," he said with a shrug but still with that wicked twinkle. "I told the travel people, don't give me no six-months-from-now-deal because I don't know if I'm going to be around then. Gimme something now."

Both of us waiting for the old elevator, the day whirled around me with sun and café con leche and piles of paper and death notices and scattered steps and little boys in Robin Hood outfits and dollar bills appearing out of nowhere and a person's life I had lived next to for years and years and years and finally got to meet.

The elevator arrived. The old doors took their usual time opening.

"Gotta do this. This trip is my last hurrah. Then I'll go quietly," Hymie said. And with that, he bump-bump-bumped his big cart of laundry into the elevator.

"MY DEUTSCHIE"

Florence's birthday. Would have been eighty-five years old.

The Ex-Lover calls.

"This is the first year your mom, my Deutschie, is not having a birthday on this earth," she says.

Except for me, there is no one she can say that to. No one. All those children she had and all her grandchildren and great-grandchildren in that small New England town—she never told them a thing.

So she calls me. The last place she has where seventy years of love is witnessed, is honored. So I listen as she once again describes the decades of speaking or not speaking, and how they both always knew the other's birthday. Cards sent, cards returned. Attempts, deep embraces, secrets, the sharing of a teenager's diary filled with longing, irreconcilable differences, marriages, divorces, and then—decades after falling in love—the miracle of a reunion, a showering of silly gifts, shared bottles of wine, and dancing naked together on secret afternoons with the blinds pulled down. And then the devastation of a breakup because neither one was willing to change their ways.

Still, at the end, Florence clutched the little guitar key chain the Ex-Lover had given her, a talisman against the encroaching darkness.

C.O. Moed

CONJUGATING LOVE

They were maybe sixteen years old and definitely not breaking up.

She had practically collapsed, looking at her iPhone.

Watching him comfort her, pushing her hair away to stroke her face, pointing down the street that spoke of a plan to make things better, hugging her, holding her when she burrowed deeper into his embrace . . .

Who says you're too young to know what love is?

You know when you put your arms around someone because you want to make it better. You know when you bury your heartbreak into those arms and feel better.

LITTLE MITZI AND THE WELBILT STOVE

"What are you doing with your mother's stove? You going to sell it?"

(Actually it was more like "Whatcha gonna do wit ya motha's stove ya gonna selit?")

Little Mitzi was finishing off a day of collecting signatures in front of Moishe's Bakery for I don't know what. We were walking back to the building she and Florence had lived in as neighbors on different floors for fifty years. She was the school aide at PS 110 when I went there.

Talking to Little Mitzi, punctuation didn't exist. At least not in the conventional way.

"I used to visit your mother we have the same stove a Welbilt I lost some knobs she said here take one of mine I said NO! what are you going to do NO! keep your knobs NO! but if you're going to sell the apartment because they don't make those knobs anymore I called they said they don't make them anymore I love my Welbilt I used to visit your mother she was lonely she told me."

I promised to give her the knobs if we ever sold the apartment. When I asked to take her picture she said "NO! I'm a very private person" and flounced out of the elevator.

C.O. Moed

THE NOT-
ON-TV OFFICE:
BEFORE AND AFTER

F ish gotta swim. Birds gotta fly. Bills gotta get paid. And they call it work for a reason.

But if you're lucky, one day you get to retire. Like Vivian. "Thirty-four years," she tells me, and then ticks off each job: "Fifteen years Dictaphone operator, you know before there were computers, eleven years regular secretary, then two years legal secretary and now, here, six years medical secretary."

That's a lot, I tell her.

"Oh. I got plans," she says.

Like what?

"I'm going to California, going see Disneyland. And then after that, I want to see what these TV shows are all about. So I'm going to *The Price Is Right*. And after that, I'm going to Chicago—*The Oprah Show*. And after that? Come back home and see Rachel Ray.

Then what? Gardening? Cruises? Volunteer work?

Vivian gives me a rare look of *Are you nuts?*

"No. After that, the college is right down the block. I'm going to learn PowerPoint and Excel. Mostly Excel. And then, I'm going to get another job."

Fish gotta swim. Birds gotta fly. Bills gotta get paid. And they call it work for a reason. Even after you retire.

THE LADIES OF THE PIZZA

Frst there was Rosy's on Pitt and Grand, the one my coworker, Annie, lived over. Then there was Aldo's on the corner of East Broadway and Grand. Now there is Pizza Shack on Columbia and Grand.

There is some other place in the middle of Grand but they also serve dogs and burgers and everything is deep-fried. If you don't want pizza, there's the luncheonette, the Chinese combo-plates-with-grease, and a sushi place. I can't imagine eating sushi on Grand Street.

Bottom line is, on Grand Street, pizza rules. Even Florence agreed with that, which is why she gave me fifty cents here and there for a slice from Aldo's. And why, years later she enjoyed a slice from the Shack on a weekly basis.

So that's why, when you're packing up your mother's life, you eat pizza. Real pizza from the Shack. Which is why I'm still not sure why I keep getting the fried-chicken-tomato pizza every day.

Today, while waiting, I mention Rosy's to Marianne and tell her about Annie living upstairs. I still dream of a meatball hero like the ones Rosy made.

(Actually, until the 1970s, Florence didn't believe in spending money for food outside the house. A bologna sandwich was it for lunch. So

C.O. Moed

I never really had a meatball hero from Rosy's, just bites offered by generous friends. Those bites were heavenly.)

Marianne not only remembers Rosy's, she tells me the family still lives in the neighborhood. Then she tells me about Rosy.

Even after they tore down the tenement and built a nice project building and new precinct on Pitt Street, Rosy still lived in the neighborhood and was a helpful neighbor. One day she decided to visit someone in Staten Island, maybe they were older or sicker than she was (she was pretty old herself at that point). So, like anyone without a car, which was just about everyone, she took the Staten Island Ferry.

Those were different times. There were no metal detectors anywhere. Shootings in schools hadn't happened yet. And if you got mugged you still had a chance to fight back.

Rosy got on the ferry. At some point, as the ferry was crossing the harbor, a guy wielding a machete started slashing people. He headed toward a young girl. He clearly was going to kill her when Rosy stepped in front of him, shielding the girl.

"She's a young girl," Rosy said. "Why are you doing this?"

He killed Rosy instead.

All I can say to Marianne is, "I'm shocked, I'm shocked, I gotta tell Annie, I'm shocked."

Since everybody knows somebody who knows everybody, we try to figure out if Annie's siblings went to PS 134 with Marianne's siblings. But mostly I'm shocked and Marianne just keeps shaking her head and repeating, "Helped everyone. He was going to kill that girl . . ."

When I ask if I can take a picture of her, Marianne says how she never likes the way she looks in pictures.

"Beautiful women never do," I tell her.

The pizza gets me through another three hours of packing.

Because on Grand Street, pizza is the bottom line and it rules these last days in Florence's home.

FLORENCE'S MOON

Keeping my head above water meant attending a much-hated yoga class.

At the beginning of every class, Teacher always played something woo-woo to lull us into thinking we would be enjoying ourselves for the next hour. Mostly it was a lot of acoustic guitars and young women's lilting voices singing of love problems that happen when you are twenty-four.

But today, instead of young angst, a solo piano rendition of "Clair de Lune" by Debussy slammed me against the wall.

I was suddenly back in a minefield packed with the millions of years I spent as a child wandering around the house listening to Florence break the heart of her piano. Until I fled at fifteen to another home, I listened to her play this piece repeatedly.

I hated this piece more than I hated yoga or practicing the violin. It was the essence of remembering that moment you had hope that love might work out, and a second later being told no, not going to happen. Those memories drown you in the worst kind of sorrow and disappointment.

Teacher began the usual blah blah blah guidance about spiritual this and intention that. But, in this class of forty or fifty people where I was the only student over the age of twenty-four, all I could see, hear, and feel was Florence the young girl and Florence the young mother and Florence the old woman playing all this hope for love she never got to keep.

C.O. Moed

STEINWAY TO HEAVEN

The Steinway Model L baby grand piano hadn't been played since the fall of 2006, when Florence could no longer sit on the hard chair, was too bewildered to read music, couldn't remember any of her repertoire, didn't have it in her to begin an eighth decade of interpreting Chopin, Debussy, Liszt, Beethoven, Brahms, Mozart, Bach . . .

. . . yeah, even Bach . . .

This Steinway was built in 1923. Florence bought it from somebody at some point in the 1940s. How a penny-pinching girl, underweight from frugal eating, could have saved up enough to buy an instrument worth thousands of dollars still puzzles my sister and me.

But, somehow, working as a waitress up in the Catskills at a bunch of Borscht Belt hotels—including the Borscht Belt hotel of all Borscht Belt hotels, Grossingers—and at a couple of nice restaurants in Greenwich Village, Florence managed to save every cent beyond the bare necessities of coffee, cigarettes, an occasional sandwich or, according to one friend, sometimes just a piece of toast to carry her from breakfast to supper.

This piano, with its sweet mellow and embracing tone, followed her everywhere, from Knickerbocker Village to Lewis Street to finally here, our family's apartment facing the Williamsburg Bridge. We think they brought the piano up six flights of stairs, the windows too small for them to hoist it up from the roof like how they do it in TV commercials or sitcoms.

When we were infants and toddlers and little kids, Florence tucked my sister or me under the Steinway so she could keep an eye on us as we napped or needed to be minded. I often crawled under there when I needed a break from the world and wanted to be close to her. I was almost a teenager when I stopped crawling under her piano as she practiced.

At some point in the 1990s, Florence had it rebuilt, which meant that after decades in the living room corner, the piano went down the stairs and back up again. Otherwise, its place in her world was as permanent as sky or sun or her fingers, which were ferocious and strong until her last breath.

It was now time to get it ready for a new life and a new corner. It was time to get it ready for new fingers.

So we called Walter. He came by as he had during Florence's last years and opened both his bag of tools and the hidden recesses of her Steinway and then cleaned out the dust and stray pens and too many paper clips and a ticker tape parade from the brittle corners of old music.

C.O. Moed

And after he was done and after years of silence, Walter's jazz poured out. Hearing the Steinway's sweet mellow and embracing tone again, I curled up where I had always curled up when that piano was being played and I just needed a break from the world.

SUNNY-SIDE UP

Kenny, the head Maintenance Guy, called, had to get in immediately because something was leaking somewhere. Luckily, I still had an emergency twenty tucked away, so I grabbed a taxi to Florence's.

(Of course, the minute I got into the cab, I could hear Florence yelling "STOP TAKING TAXIS!" To which I yelled back "YOU'RE DEAD!! LEAVE ME ALONE ALREADY!!")

However, the dashing driver was not dead and he and I started chatting about the decrease of taxi use and the possibility of driving a bus. He asked what I did.

"I'm an obscure writer with a day job."

"Oh! You can write about me."

So I took a picture and, handing him my card, told him to check the blog in a couple of days.

"I don't just drive a taxi." And he handed me his card. There, dashing smile and all, was his picture next to bright bold letters announcing SUNNYSIDE REAL ESTATE: *All Your Residential and Business Needs Met!*

"You're like in the two worst professions to be in during a recession," I said in disbelief.

He laughed, said, "What can you do? You work."

Knocked down seven.

Get up eight.

C.O. Moed

Everybody called her the Phone Lady.

Going from public phone to public phone, she'd pick up the receiver and start screaming her end of a conversation she was in the middle of with someone. Screaming. Like the Flood but no Ark.

She had regular rounds up and down Grand Street. Nobody stopped her or asked her why. Or anything. We all just stood there and watched or walked by.

After screaming her side of things for about five minutes, she'd then take the receiver and repeatedly slam it down.

Bang

Bash bash bash

Bang

Like a parent raining down a billion fists upon an errant child because they didn't give the right answer.

Bang

Bash bash bash

Bang

Then she'd walk to the next public pay phone. And the next and the next and the next.

A day or so later, the telephone repair guy would quietly retrace her footsteps and, like a social worker, gently fix each phone back into some working order.

A day or a week or a couple of hours later the Phone Lady would return and it would all begin again.

HYMIE COMES TO VISIT

The painting behind Hymie is a 1950 painting of the Williamsburg Bridge by William Chaiken who, around five a.m. every morning, used to shovel coal into the Henry Street Music School furnace while Florence snuck in a private practice session to tackle Beethoven and Chopin before everyone woke up. When I was recently in touch with William, he described it as having a private concert every day.

Signs in all the buildings begin with "Furniture for Free . . ." and end with ". . . a bit dusty."

A lot of people come by for the furniture and sundry household and office items. But a couple of them want to see what Florence had that they don't—maybe more rooms, more light, a better view of the Williamsburg Bridge.

Hymie stops by to see if there is any furniture left. But mostly he wants to talk about the broken front lobby door.

"A junkie did it! Only this building. It was a junkie. From the other side of the bridge," he insists. He is sure of it.

"No, it was revenge against the board member who lives on the [such-and-such] floor. *That's* why it's always this building," I insist. I am sure of it.

"Obama! But I don't like he wants to talk to Iran."

C.O. Moed

"Hymie, dialogue creates peace. War hasn't ever worked out."

I don't know what happened in the POW camp he was in, but his face gets this very far-away look. "What if they don't wanna talk?" he shoots back.

"Then you talk anyways!"

He changes the subject. They took all the furniture? Did we have any records or tapes? He likes music. I promise to bring him the jazz cassette tapes I had just taken home.

"I got tons of tapes. Here, come on. I'll show you."

And for the first time ever in fifty years of my family living in this building, I go visit Hymie's home and see all his paintings, his real kaleidoscope, and his many, many tapes of just about everyone—Ella, Duke, Coltrane, Sinatra, Torme, Basie, Getz, more Ella . . .

He points to his kitchen sideboard. "Gotta paint that."

"Have Jimmy the Maintenance Guy do that. Ten dollars, *boom*, it's done."

"Nah. I can do it."

Later, I run into him coming back into the lobby carrying a new can of paint. Over his shoulder he says, "It was the fire department. They broke the lobby door."

WHAT A WARRIOR LOOKS LIKE

I decided to try a new yoga class. Stepping into the room, I saw only one other young woman, and she looked at least thirty-five. Everyone else looked like eighty.

This nine a.m. class is going to be a snap, I thought to myself. Especially after the teacher said in her best kindergarten voice, "Class is starting. Class is starting," and everyone kept on gossiping and catching up on all the health problems they were all having.

Things began slow and easy enough. And I was feeling all smug and stuff when suddenly thirty-odd women, with a fierceness that only comes from surviving old age, stepped forward like an army emerging from a fog, ready to do battle.

These were warriors never seen in Hollywood blockbuster movies or action comic books.

These were warriors who had no holiday on a Monday or a statue in a big park.

These were warriors I could barely keep up with.

Finally, the end of class was near. The teacher, in her best kindergarten voice, asked, "Is there any pose you'd like to do?"

"Side plank," someone called out.

Are you fucking kidding me? I thought to myself. Side plank was what I watched skinny, healthy eighteen-year-old girls straight out of athletic-wear catalogs do on yoga DVDs.

C.O. Moed

A woman near me said, "Oh, I can't do that."

"Me neither," I told her.

"Knee operation," she said.

"Me too!" (Yeah, so what if it was a year ago.)

The teacher, in her best kindergarten voice, began instructing.

And once again, that army of warriors, including the woman who just had a knee operation, rose up out of a fog made from my disbelief.

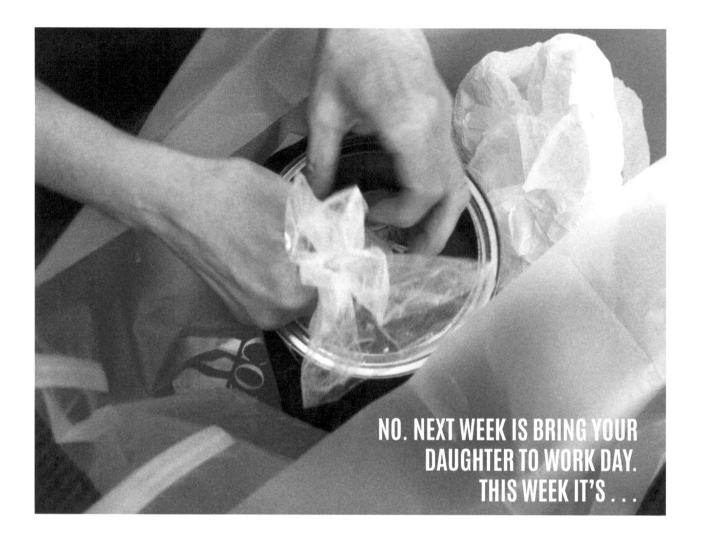

NO. NEXT WEEK IS BRING YOUR
DAUGHTER TO WORK DAY.
THIS WEEK IT'S . . .

The only time we could pick up, well, I'm not exactly sure what or how to call it—the remains of Florence? Mom-in-a-Can? Chock-Full-of-Ashes?—the only time we could pick up the aforementioned from the nonprofit full-service funeral place was eight a.m. to three p.m.

I offered to do it before work, because a whole pictorial unfolded before my eyes.

Bring Your Dead Mom to Work Day!

I'd put the can by the computer or next to all the reports, or maybe on top of the file cabinet by all the reference books. If I thought I could get away with it, I'd even do a series of "Mom on the escalator"!

So I was very disappointed when my sister Louise took the day off, picked her up, brought her back to the family apartment and stored her under the Steinway—the very place Florence put us from the moment we were born until we got too big and too old to want to hang around her feet.

That entire space under the piano was filled with boxes of music theory and history books—Beethoven's contrapuntal harmonies,

　　　　　　　　　　　　　　C.O. Moed

religion and Bach's fugal textures, Clara Schuman and the modern piano—and now a very lovely plastic bag holding a very lovely velveteen bag: Mom.

Each time we went down there, we'd forget that was her, and wonder what that bag was for.

Finally my sister said, "I want to look. I think it's important to look."

We looked.

"Stop moving so much," I ordered. "You have such pretty hands."

"It's not her," my sister stated.

Honestly, how could you tell? Then I realize she was talking concept.

The Internet search about what one does with a can of Mom let us know that our plan of surreptitiously dumping her at Coney Island, although truly the most honoring thing to do:

(a) was against the law; and

(b) ran the risk of having recognizable pieces of bones surprise dogs and swimmers.

That left me putting it in the high closet next to her reel-to-reel tapes, or my sister burying her in her backyard. "What will it do to my plants?" ended that option.

Florence went back under the piano.

I wonder where Gramma is.

SAME PARK

DIFFERENT REASON TO RUN FAST

I t was a perfect night to take a stroll.

Sauntering into Bryant Park, I marveled at the couples hanging about, the concession stand looking like a café in a French movie and all these folding chairs around for people to sit and enjoy.

I still don't understand how come no one steals them.

Walking past a bunch of trees, there were suddenly several Ping-Pong tables and a whole lot of guys with paddles hanging about, waiting patiently.

Like Mr. Godslove.

"I'm an OK Ping-Pong player," he says.

Mr. Godslove is from Nigeria. He is living here in New York with his mother. She had been a very successful milliner in Nigeria and they would go back in a heartbeat, except . . . He stopped there and we all understood. Sometimes home is not a safe place to be.

Here in New York, Mr. Godslove was getting ready to go to APEX to study automotive stuff. Meanwhile, as he waited for school to start, he hung out at Bryant Park, waiting for his turn to play Ping-Pong all night.

We watched the game—lots of running and dashing and jumping and slamming.

C.O. Moed

"I used to work on Fortieth Street many years ago. There was no Ping-Pong then," I told Mr. Godslove.

No indeed. There wasn't much of anything, except for a lot—a lot—of bad, bad, bad people either doing a lot of drugs, selling a lot of drugs, or taking a break from mugging passersby.

In the middle of this dangerous land there was one deserted walking path between Fortieth Street, where the office was, and Forty-Second Street, where the old Irish bar was. It served Happy Hour from four to six, and had little hot dogs and other cute things to eat for dinner.

At four, especially on Thursdays and Fridays when we got paid, all of us office girls—most of the young ones and every single one of the old ones, including Mary who was easily seventy—we'd make a wild dash from the Fortieth Street side of Bryant Park to the Forty-Second Street side. For someone not quite five feet tall and about three feet wide, Mary could run.

Yeah. In those days, there were no pretty chairs, no café, no cute couples, no Ping-Pong table—no nothing.

And there was no Mr. Godslove, shyly beaming as he described how he worked hard to be an OK Ping-Pong player.

SHE'S LEAVING HOME

One day, Florence's piano left the building.

For good.

My sister Louise had found a community center in Bensonhurst with an active classical music school. That felt right. After all, Brooklyn became home to Florence and her mother, Sophie, when the money ran out.

Who knows . . . maybe some kid will sit down at those keys and, like Florence, begin decades of interpreting Chopin, Debussy, Liszt, Beethoven, Brahms, Mozart, Bach . . .

. . . yeah, even Bach . . .

An Account of the Day by Louise

Two men were at the bottom end of the piano going down the stairs . . .

C.O. Moed

. . . and the third man was at the top of the piano pulling up, preventing all the weight of the piano from being on the two men underneath.

That was so clever. It reminded me of the 1964 movie Topkapi about a jewel heist in Turkey—the scene where Peter Ustinov holds the acrobat up from the roof of the museum. I couldn't stop talking about it for the rest of the day.

I was already back at the office when the mover called to tell me they left their dolly on the sidewalk on Broome Street.

I no longer carry the courtyard security office phone number as I used to when Florence was alive, and I didn't even remember the name of the head Maintenance Guy. I hadn't even run into anyone from Maintenance or Security when I arrived or while we moved the piano out.

It took a while for me to figure out how to get the number of the security office, but somehow I located it. So I called up.

"Hi. I moved a piece of furniture this morning and the mover left a dolly . . ."

"Oh yes, you're Claire's sister and you moved the piano out of A51 this morning. Kenny has the dolly right here."

I was astounded. I didn't notice anyone noticing us.

I wish there had been a security office with people who knew us when we were kids instead of Hartman, the cop, a gruff old portly man who walked around the courtyard glowering at anyone under five feet tall.

It felt pretty wonderful that today Ms. King in the security office knew the comings and goings of Florence's piano.

AN UNEXPECTED DAY

In the middle of everything, an unexpected writing grant came through. Suddenly, I could face each day, at least for a little while, without that familiar terror of shattering into eviction and homelessness. Suddenly, I could do what I had trained for—stay home and write full time.

To get used to time that I suddenly owned, I took myself for a walk. Sitting in the front window of a "European" fast-food place, I stared out the window and pondered the truism "the secret is in the sauce," because the only thing making it possible to chew and swallow the veggie hot dog was the relish, ketchup, and mustard.

No matter the bad food. It was such a rare and unexpected relief to feel safe in an unanchored world.

Then she sat down.

C.O. Moed

So, I watched her watch.

And watch.

And watch.

Finally she headed to parts unknown.

She slowly faded into the Twenty-Third Street crowds, and I wondered if she lived with familiar fears like mine or if, on this rare day, was also enjoying unexpected relief.

C.O. Moed

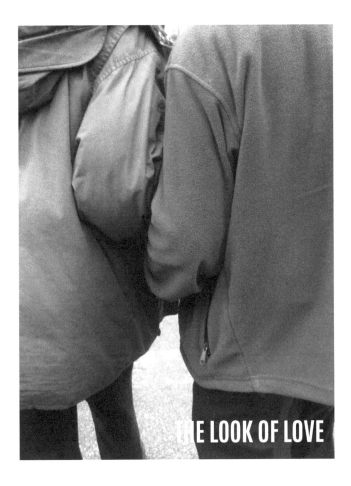

THE LOOK OF LOVE

They both are wearing the same soft outdoorsy clothes, and their shoes are sturdy and hardy and probably very, very comfortable, and the only difference between them are the colors of their soft and comfy attire.

She strides ahead to the corner to wait for the light to change, and he comes up behind her and gives her a gentle nudge. Hello, his elbow says to hers. Hello, I've caught up with you.

And she turns and smiles and he grins back at her and I see billions of seconds and minutes and moments and days and years they have shared together, traveled through together, survived together.

No matter where they are, they get to turn and see the other who has caught up. Together they get to patiently wait for life or news or even the walk signal to change.

Nobody notices them because they are too old to look like TV love. Love on TV only happens between the ages of fifteen and twenty-two. Sometimes thirty. Occasionally forty. Never eighty.

I follow them for blocks because I want to see what the future could look like.

THE EYE OF THE BEHOLDER
IS NOT FOR THE SQUEAMISH

Today will be the last time I think Florence is looking at me.

The upheaval of emptying closets and preparing to vacate the apartment unearthed the bag of her glass eye and its paraphernalia that I had stuffed into a corner hoping it would disappear on its own.

The only time things disappear on their own is when you are looking for them. The things you want to forget stay stubbornly in place waiting to piss you off and freak you out.

How to explain this piece of glass except to say it isn't one. It is, if anything, the portrait of my mother, still as vibrantly alive as when it resided in her empty socket.

As a little girl, I didn't know this eye couldn't see. All I knew was that Florence slept facing her bedroom's doorway with one eye half opened. I thought it was to make sure I didn't slip past her on my illegal expeditions around the house after bedtime and before breakfast. I liked the house when nobody was up. Unlike the angry silences or not-so-silent anger when folks were up, before breakfast and after bedtime offered rare peace and a world of possibilities. Worth the risk.

Peeking into my parents' bedroom, I'd stare back at her, and if she didn't say anything I'd wave, just to make sure she wasn't seeing me scoot past her and into wonderful, quiet, empty rooms.

My illicit activities didn't end there. One day, left alone in the apartment while she and my father were out and about, I, desperate to understand yet another angry silence between them, went through all their drawers and closets. Spying two beautiful ring boxes in Florence's underwear drawer (right next to an odd disc made of rubber), I eagerly opened one, hoping for something special.

There she was, staring back at me.

On walks home from TV night at Gramma's in Knickerbocker Village, my sister and I would ask, "What happened to your eye?" But Florence never answered. She'd just glower and continue striding down Madison Street. Later, my father would tell us her father, whom she never spoke to, said she was born with something wrong, and that she was in the hospital a long time and not allowed to see her mother. Hospitals did that in those days. Fearing it would be injurious to the little kids to be with their families, parents weren't allowed to visit their children for months.

But, years and years and years after that, putting out the fires dementia makes, for some reason I had to call the place that made her eye. So, while I had them on the phone, I asked, "Do you know what happened to her eye?"

"Well, she said it was a gunshot accident," they told me.

I think she was pulling their leg. Although it was plausible. Florence spoke of her neighbors in Bushwick, Brooklyn, knitting hunting mittens.

The Ex-Lover told me that when they first met, she didn't even know that eye was glass. All she knew was Florence's hair hid half her face. Just introduced but knowing something different was happening, she pushed the hair to the side and told Florence, "You look better this way."

There were also gentle moments of care when, in public, one of us daughters would whisper "Wipe your eye" if it got too cloudy. But that was as close as my sister or I ever got to Florence even admitting there was anything wrong. Even at the emergency room of the Eye and Ear Hospital at 2:30 in the morning, it was I who had to tell the attending doctor the eye that didn't have cataracts was glass. Florence just sat there tight-lipped and furious that he dared to even investigate.

She was so determined to defy and deny her lack of sight, that, when coming home from an operation on her one good eye that was completely bandaged up, she pushed my hand away as we entered the apartment complex and pretended she was seeing through her glass eye as she walked blindly to her lobby door.

However, that last year of her life changed everything. Florence began asking me if her eye was OK and could I fix it? After fifty years of that piece of glass being a wall between us, putting her eye into her empty socket and adjusting it was probably the most loving thing I have ever done for her. The Rubicon had been crossed. By both of us.

Today, I will bring this portrait of my mother over to the Eye and Ear Hospital where it will be donated to a project that refits glass eyes for those in need.

But before I do, I will look my mother in the eye for the last time and for the last time I will think my mother is looking back at me.

FOOD, LIES AND EATING WELL

Irene and I touch base. Her mother had a fall but is doing OK for now. Irene, on the other hand, is swamped with caretaking. The strategy I used on Florence—reassuring and agreeing—is definitely helping her get through the day.

Except for the issue of food. "I always offer to buy my mom food that she would enjoy," Irene writes in her email. "However, she refuses and insists on getting free food from the neighborhood senior food program, but she only marginally enjoys those meals. She would prefer to eat fish and beef prepared Cantonese-style, but there's no way that would be free. At her age she should be enjoying what she eats, but she won't take anything that isn't free. It's gotta be because of the aftermath of the Chinese-Japanese war when she was a child."

Oh, the fear there isn't enough money for food because of war, because of the Great Depression, because of poverty, because of . . .

There was only one thing to do when faced with an old person refusing to spend money on good food. Lie, I write Irene. Lie. I told Florence I was getting all this free food from the government because she was losing too much weight. So she started eating again. Lie and tell your mom that the Chinatown Alliance opened a free food program for seniors.

"Oh Claire," Irene writes back. "You don't understand the power of Chinese networking. My mom just has to mention it to one person how delicious the food was and direct that one person to Chinatown Alliance and sooner than you can say Chinatown Alliance, Chinatown Alliance would have a line snaking around the corner. And then Chinatown Alliance would put out a wanted poster for the morally depraved Jewish chick who told a lie."

Well, I've always wanted to be wanted.

REMAINS OF THE DAY

Florence's cedar boxes. From Coney Island, the beach towns of New Jersey, and one from Seneca Lake in upstate New York. Snapshots of rare travels away from the Lower East Side and proof money had been spent on something unnecessary.

These little boxes lined the top of Florence's bureaus for as long as I could remember. Filled with small treasures and precious mementos. Like a photo-booth picture of her with the Ex-Lover.

These are where she kept her hopes, her dreams, her secret self. But when I look at them now, I just see empty boxes. Not her silver-white hair that exploded beauty and defied convention. Not her whirling about in a good foxtrot with a fine woman. Not her hands, that last year of life, seeking someone to hold them.

THE ERASER

"It's history. It's precious history! PLEASE, don't destroy her letters to you!"

I'd be screaming this, but I am trying calm negotiation and polite words first. Still, I'm gritting my teeth so hard I'm surprised I can even get words out.

The Ex-Lover pulls her *Who's Who in America* voice that has voted Republican in every single election—has voted repeatedly against love like hers and Florence's—that voice—and she says again: "They're private."

"PLEASE. Reconsider. Donate them. Donate the letters to the Lesbian Herstory Archives with a rule they can't be read for a hundred years. Or send them to me. Send them to me and I'll keep them safe."

But behind my attempt at calm negotiations, behind every polite word, behind gritted teeth, I'm begging, begging, silently ranting . . .

. . . please don't erase my mother's love for you please she lived broken and unloved in how she was meant to be loved please don't erase the one place she fought for when you two were young and bursting with an excitement you had no name for on your first bike ride to Coney Island it was Rosh Hashanah it was our New Year's you were barely seventeen but you knew you knew you found each other please don't erase that moment that hope that place you told her to leave you told her to leave and go and get married you were both going to get married and stop this foolishness please don't erase the place she found again reclaimed again after all those decades living in silent rage and loss and hate for giving up what she was supposed to be because you told her to go live frozen dead in a life of husband and kids she finally broke free of broke free fifty-eight years old strode down the street on Gay Pride Day with a swagger that only comes from loving girls again . . .

Please.

Don't do to her what you did to yourself lying to your children and your grandchildren and your great-grandchildren like you were a paragon of a respectable life you secretly hated missing every day the love of your life you missed her love every day of your life you missed Florence every hour of every day of your . . .

"They're private," the Ex-Lover says again. And with that she rings off never to speak to me again.

C.O. Moed

t is time.

There is nothing much left to do.

Outside it pours cold rain. Inside all the boxes filled with Florence's home have been tucked into my sister Louise's and my old childhood bedroom—the bedroom Florence moved into after shaking off an unhappy marriage and a suffocating life.

Once she settled into that old bedroom, Florence never slept anywhere else, with the exception of two occasions. A brief period in 1976 when she camped out on the living room couch after one of us daughters accidentally returned home. And one late night, a year ago.

For some reason I was in the house, fixing something or other. Penny came in. "Florence is in my bed and won't leave."

Sure enough, there was Florence, back in her old marital bedroom, curled up in one of our childhood single beds that Penny and Gabriella now took turns sleeping on.

"This is my home," Florence stated, refusing to budge.

Penny looked exhausted. And we both knew forcing her wouldn't work.

HOME AWAITS

DIASPORA BEGINS

I started gently cooing, "This is where you slept when you were very unhappy. This was a very unhappy place for you. Let's go back to the bed where you are happy. Your happy bed."

And holding hands, she and I walked back to her own bed where, after that unhappy marriage, her joys and her sorrows were her own.

Now what is left of my mother's joys and sorrows—her ashes and her dust—lie in a cardboard can in my big satchel, nestled between leftover sandwich bags and the old mirror that she used to scrutinize her hand technique at her piano.

There are numbers on the lid of the can, and like any good Jew I think of the concentration camps. The distillation of a person into a number.

Buried under a huge knapsack and a ton of bags packed to the gills, I rush into the hard rain and get to the corner of Columbia and Grand, only to watch a rare Avenue A bus fly by. Looking down under the Bridge, there's no Avenue D bus waiting to go. At eleven p.m. there won't be any more buses for a long, long while.

Until gentrification there were no cabs on Grand Street, ever. Never, ever, ever. Yet there is a silver lining to the influx of the new residents buying at market value, because suddenly—right in front of me—there is a shiny empty taxi.

Before Florence's ghost could give me any shit, I put my foot down. "I DON'T WANNA HEAR IT. IT'S LATE. I'M TAKING IT."

Sometimes you just gotta draw the line somewhere.

As we barrel up Essex Street, I look at the name of the driver. Mr. A is from Togo. He hasn't been home in five years. It is very difficult being so far away from his family, he tells me. Things aren't good there. And here he is studying mathematics at Columbia University. But yes it is hard. He misses home.

The way he says *home* and *miss* and *family* shreds what's left of my heart.

At the same time that Florence packed up her ability to walk and her will to live, I lost the man I loved, the one I believed I would build a home with, share his family with, the man I thought I would live with until death do us part.

After his sudden goodbye, I crawled through those bad weekday nights and brutal weekend afternoons and I made myself think of my grandmother who, at seventeen, got on a ship and fled to America, never to see her mother or her favorite brother ever again. And I'd

C.O. Moed

remind myself, "Who the hell am I to think I am excused from Diaspora? Who the hell am I?"

We leave our homes in boats and planes and taxis and cardboard cans with a bunch of numbers on the top. We leave with hope or in terror. We leave with our hearts broken or our hearts bursting.

But we leave.

The rain pours down. Light skitters across wet streets. Traffic signals change.

Diaspora begins.

V CODA

IN THE STILL OF A NEW NIGHT

Long ago, only rich people living in fancy apartments had air conditioners. We weren't and we didn't. So, during hot summer days and nights, Florence, along with all the neighbors, would prop open her front door and hope for a breeze to waft in from the stairwell's window facing Columbia Street.

From all those many opened doors, all those different lives would weave in and out of this village of thirty-five apartments, filling the halls with television commercials, occasional conversations shouted from room to room, and the smells of a billion things cooking for Shabbos or Sunday dinner.

One late, late night recently, during a heat wave that had gone on for days and with only a tiny air conditioner in the bedroom, I checked to make sure the building was sleeping and there were no neighbors about. I propped open my front door in hope of relief.

A breeze blew in from the airshaft. And as it did, the cat ran out, unable to resist the cool of hundred-year-old marble floors. I tried to catch him until, feeling better for the first time in days, I realized he had a good point.

Soon, after checking the coast was clear, I, like Florence, began opening my front door into the deep cool night. The cat and I wandered the stairs, listening to our neighbors sleep and humming along with all the air conditioners in the airshaft. And after our stroll, the two of us sat in the empty stairwell.

I miss the normalcy of open doors during hot days and sleepless nights. And when my door is closed because the neighbors are awake, I miss my mother.

C.O. Moed

PRIDE MAKES THE FUTURE

can't
break
this

When the right to love is at stake, it doesn't matter what shoes you march in. The blisters can wait until tomorrow. Today your feet are flying across all the no-you-cant's. Because YES YOU CAN.

YES mends every heartbreak. YES offers up more love than anyone could ever have imagined possible. YES makes a heart indestructible.

And to the Ex-Lover, who lives alone in a small town in another state and has loved Florence all her life but whose children, grandchildren, great-grandchildren do not know the multi-colors of her heart, a Happy Pride to you.

You couldn't live in a world made of your love. But everyone is marching now so that this little boy can live in a world where no one has to hide their heart ever again.

C.O. Moed

BLESSED JOURNEY, SAFE TRAVELS

Even though she had just pulled away from the curb, that bus driver opened the door for the once-young and running-as-fast-as-he-could gentleman.

The entire way uptown she said hello to passengers, telling the woman with the cane to take her time, patiently answering the girl who was carrying on a simultaneous conversation on her cell phone about what stop was best to get to the hospital.

And when the elderly man got caught smack in the middle of the crosswalk at Third Street just as the light changed, she called out to the crossing guard, "Let him cross, let him cross."

And then she waited, because a light turning green or red was not as important as an elderly man who clearly couldn't walk faster than really slow, but who needed to get to the other side of the street.

And because the bus driver told the crossing guard to let him cross, the crossing guard went out into the middle of the street, held up five lanes of traffic and guided that old man safely to the corner.

Watching her, I remembered all the people who helped Florence as she stumbled through a city she once ruled, one that was suddenly beyond her disappearing capabilities.

All the bus drivers, train conductors, fellow passengers, passerby-ers, deli guys, coffee shop owners, that night at the hospital when Maria fed her. All our fellow New Yorkers, all our city's heart and soul, all our love. All our New York . . .

"God is good," the bus driver told me as I got off the bus.

"So are you," I answered.

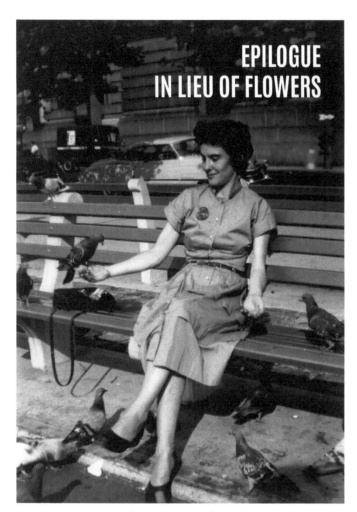

EPILOGUE
IN LIEU OF FLOWERS

Tell the truth.
Tell yourself the truth.

Don't let the bullshit you believe compromise either of the above.

Don't lie. Unless you're drunk. Then really don't lie.

Don't steal.

Accept hand-me-downs.

Look fabulous in your own clothes. They may have started out as hand-me-downs, but they're yours now. Proudly recount their lineage. Never feel ashamed about that.

Never take a taxi.

Walk everywhere.

Don't wear a coat in winter.

Carry your own weight to the point of pathology. Better to err on independence than not.

Refuse to lose at the hands of cowardliness, mediocrity, stupidity, and the need to blend in.
Suffer aloneness at the risk of fitting in with any of the above.

Refuse to feel fear. If you do, ignore it and keep going. Just like Florence did that night during a World War II blackout under the Manhattan Bridge by the movie theater (now a Chinese market).

Always put your work first.
Always do your work.
Always put your work first.
Always do your work.

C.O. Moed

Rage against the machine. Even when it looks like it's related to you.

Risk being laughed at by morons when you do something no one else is doing. Just like when Florence put on those roller skates in 1972 and skated up and down Grand Street and all those people laughed at her and then a couple of years later everyone had disco skates.

Start your entire life over at fifty-eight like you are a fourteen-year-old. Because on some level, you still are.

Fight back just like Florence did all the times someone mugged her or tried to mug her during the 1970s.

Don't *ever* quit.

Know that that beer, that sandwich, those shoes, that jacket, those pants, that avenue, that movie house, that proper grammar, that etude, that sonata, that scale, that subway, that bus, that street, that bar, that woman, that dance, that hot dog, that boardwalk, that beach, that ocean is Your New York.

IT WAS HERS.

This is the bakery I'd stop in after a day with Florence.

On her last Saturday alive, I pried my fingers out of her tightly held grasp and told her I had to go. She begged me to stay. Just a little bit longer. But I had nothing left inside. I needed to go home to nothing so I could start all over again. So, I said what I knew she'd absolutely understand. I said I had to go home and work.

"Go. Go do your work," she said, letting go of my fingers.

She said it the way she taught me to say it. Your Work was more important than anything. It was more important than love or family or illness or even death. In fact, when her mother, Sophie died, Florence delayed all the necessary next steps one must take after someone dies because she was inundated with rehearsals and teaching and helping my sister prepare for her senior recital at City College.

That last Saturday with Florence was balmy so I got what I always get at this bakery on Grand Street: one pork bun and a cup of tea with milk and sugar. Then I sat in Chrystie Park and watched all the men I always saw on TV but never grew up with run up and down the soccer field.

C.O. Moed

Florence died two days later.

For months, I repeatedly asked myself if I could have stayed longer.

A Dutch friend who is a funeral director called one day to see how I was doing. "Don't chew," she instructed. Don't go over minute by minute and detail by detail wondering *if* . . .

Don't chew. There were many cows in her country so that analogy made sense.

Now, lovely people are looking to live in Florence's old home. An irreversible process has begun.

I returned to a home that didn't look like the one I grew up in. It was painted and polished and nicely appointed. It was like meeting a ghost that looked much, much better dead than when it had been alive.

At some point it was time to go. But instead of heading home to nothing, I headed to the Staten Island Ferry where a kinder night and a bed I couldn't have dreamt of in my millions of nights of insomnia awaited me. I had, after decades of searching, finally found new love. I could see what my future looked like.

On the way, I stopped in at the bakery. It was not an homage or nostalgia. It was simply what one did after such trips.

The weather too rainy and cold, I sat inside with my usual cup of tea and pork bun and listened to a gaggle of men talk, laugh, argue, and, from what I could tell, check the racing sheets. Their chatter of Tagalog, Cantonese, and English felt like Christmas lights to me—bright and dancing.

One day in 2006, I started writing the city I knew as intimately as I knew Florence. And I found I barely knew either. When you are home, when you are in a family, it is normal like breathing, and yet mysterious like prayer.

As I walked with Florence to where she needed to go, and as I continued on without her, the urgency I felt to witness and document and make sure I honored the New York we both knew as intimately as breathing and as mysterious as prayer only grew fiercer.

It is not nostalgia for the good old days. Because they weren't. It is, simply, what one does when telling the story of home.

Acknowledgments

It Was Her New York is excerpted from myprivateconey.blogspot.com (2006–2018).

"A Night at the ER" was published in *Thorn Literary Magazine*, 2020 Bonus Edition.

An excerpt of *It Was Her New York* was published in *Inspirational Art Magazine*, June 2022.

ACKNOWLEDGEMENTS, aka IT TAKES A &$*#$&ING VILLAGE
Thanks to editor Deborah Heimann, photo editor consultant Ted Krever, story consultant Camilla Saly, copy editor Marisa Keller, photographer Morgan Gwenwald, publicist Louise O'Brien, designer Sienna Long, Eddie Vincent of ENC Graphics, and Samantha Kolber of Rootstock Publishing.

Thanks to all the participants and contributors for so generously sharing their stories:

Louise A. Moed, Judith Bloch, Giselaine Carrington, Nick Clement, Marianne Ferrara, Mr. Godslove, Hyman Siegel (RIP), Mr. E from Ghana, Adriene Johnson (RIP), Ann Kelly, Toby Levy, Irene Ong, Laurel Rosenzweig-Hirsch, LaTanya Waluyn, Theresa Williams, Joni Wong, the New York Sparrow, Mr. Sunnyside Real Estate, and Mr. A. of Togo.

Thank you to all the first readers who helped bring *Her New York* to life: Ramona Clay Alexander, Judith Bloch, Wendy Caster, Dave "Dash" Delano, Elizabeth DeNoma, Isabelle Dupuis, Adrian Garcia Gomez, Christiaan Lampinen, Elisabeth Lohninger, Christine Mahon, Damani Moyd, Robin Nagle, Rob Nietupski, Stephanie Salt, Doug Shapiro, and Katherine Stephan.

Thank you for all the love and support along the way: Stewart Ansel, Madeline Artenberg, Sherry Armenstein, Shawn Cowls, Noemi De LaCruz, Carola Dibbell, Deb Edel, Pearline Edwards, Amy Ferris, Nicole Frail, Philip Giambri, Amy Gladstone, Helene Granqvist, Paula Grant, Ed Hamilton, Yolande Heijnen, D. John Hopper, Ben Joseph, Mimi Keghida, Linda Kleinbub, David Kosky, David Leaf, Elisabeth Lohninger, Josslyn Luckett, Debbie Martin, Rebecca Marx, Amy Meadow, Prince N. McNally, Jeremiah Moss, Anthony Murphy, Nurit Nardi, Joan Nestle, John Nyamu, Joke Peters, Valeria Richter, Uliana Salerno, Peggy Shaw, Maureen Slattery, Kristi Sunde, Samantha Talbot, Joel Anderson Thompson, Celeste Wade, Ruth Wyatt, David N. Zimmer, my Soka Gakkai community, and my Monday night friends.

Special thanks to: Ellen Polivy; Dr. Valerie Portnoi and his staff; everyone at Beth Israel Hospital's emergency room; everyone who helped me at all the Medicaid, CASA II, and Social Security offices; all the FDNY EMTs and private EMTs who ferried Florence back and forth; Daytop Village colleagues and management; and all the visitors to myprivateconey.blogspot.com.

Special gratitude to Joni Wong for her never-ending, constant friendship, support, and belief in my work, and for her friendship with Florence (you were always her favorite).

All my love and gratitude to my partner-in-crime and muse, Ted Krever, who doesn't just bring me coffee every morning, but whose fierce brilliance and strong opinions have made this a better book. Without your love and support, none of this could have happened.

PHOTO CREDITS

All photos by C.O. Moed, or from family albums and used by permission, with the exception of the following:

Page 13, PROMISED LAND: Photographer: F.D Moed, Moed Archives, Used by Permission.

Page 37, DISCIPLES OF DISCIPLINE: Photographer: Mr. Schindelheim, Moed Archives, Used by Permission.

Page 59, FROM THAT MOMENT ON: Photographer: F.D Moed, Moed Archives, Used by Permission.

Page 62 GIRLS NEXT DOOR PHOTO ALBUM: Photographer: Wittmyers Picture Studio, Used by Permission of Laurel Rosenzweig-Hirsch.

Page 63-64, DELANCEY STREET, FAMILY, HERMAN, DELI GUY: Unknown photographer, Used by Permission of Laurel Rosenzweig-Hirsch.

Page 66-67, LATANYA: HEAVY LIFTING and SELF-PORTRAIT: Photographer: Latanya Waluyn, Used by Permission.

Page 75, WHEN US THREE WENT A-TRAVELING: Photographer: F.D Moed, Moed Archives, Used by Permission.

Page 80, ON THE BORDER OF DESTITUTE: Photographer: Sophie Deutsch, Moed Archives, Used by Permission.

Page 148-149, SHE'S LEAVING HOME: Photographer: Louise Moed, Used by Permission.

Page 166, PRIDE MAKES THE FUTURE: FLORENCE AND SAGE: Photographer: Morgan Gwenwald, Used by Permission.

Page 172, IT WAS HER NEW YORK ACKNOWLEDGEMENTS: Photographer: Joni Wong, Used by Permission.

About the Author

C.O. Moed grew up on New York's Lower East Side when it was still a tough neighborhood. A recipient of the Elizabeth George Grant for Fiction, Rockefeller Media Arts nominee, and an alum of the infamous and groundbreaking WOW Café, her work has appeared in various presses and anthologies, including the *Silver-Tongued Devil Anthology*; *Lilith Magazine*, *Shades of Blue* (Seal Press), *Sensitive Skin*, *Unexpected Stories*, *100subtexts magazine*, *Inspirational Art Magazine*, and *AWAKE!: Reader for the Sleepless* (Soft Skull Press).

Moed explores the elusive definition of home, chronicling stories of family, neighbors, and the city through writing and street photography. She lives with fellow writer Ted Krever and a cat. They are all Mets fans.

🍃 More Nonfiction from Rootstock Publishing:

A Peek Under the Hood: Heroin, Hope, & Operation Tune-Up by Michael Pevarnik

A Judge's Odyssey by Dean B. Pineles

A Lawyer's Life to Live by Kimberly B. Cheney

Alzheimer's Canyon: One Couple's Reflections on Living with Dementia by Jane Dwinell & Sky Yardley

Attic of Dreams: A Memoir by Marilyn Webb Neagley

Catalysts for Change ed. by Doug Wilhelm

China in Another Time by Claire Malcolm Lintilhac

Circle of Sawdust: A Circus Memoir of Mud, Myth, Mirth, Mayhem and Magic by Rob Mermin

Collecting Courage: Anti-Black Racism in the Charitable Sector eds. Nneka Allen, Camila Vital Nunes Pereira, & Nicole Salmon

Cracked: My Life After a Skull Fracture by Jim Barry

I Could Hardly Keep From Laughing by Don Hooper & Bill Mares

Nobody Hitchhikes Anymore by Ed Griffin-Nolan

Notes from the Porch: Tiny True Stories to Make You Feel Better about the World by Thomas Christopher Greene

Pauli Murray's Revolutionary Life by Simki Kuznick

Preaching Happiness by Ginny Sassaman

Red Scare in the Green Mountains by Rick Winston

Save Me a Seat! A Life with Movies by Rick Winston

Snapshots of a Life: Essays by Ken Libertoff

Striding Rough Ice: Coaching College Hockey and Growing Up In the Game by Gary Wright

Tales of Bialystok: A Jewish Journey from Czarist Russia by Charles Zachariah Goldberg

The Atomic Bomb on My Back by Taniguchi Sumiteru

The Language of Liberty by Edwin C. Hagenstein

The Last Garden by Liza Ketchum

The Morse Code: Legacy of a Vermont Sportswriter by Brendan Buckley

Uncertain Fruit: A Memoir of Infertility, Loss, and Love by Rebecca & Sallyann Majoya

Walking Home: Trail Stories by Celia Ryker

You Have a Hammer: Building Grant Proposals for Social Change by Barbara Floersch

Learn about our Fiction, Poetry, and Children's titles at www.rootstockpublishing.com.

Printed in the USA
CPSIA information can be obtained
at www.ICGtesting.com
LVHW060422010224
770415LV00001B/1